Reviving the Love for Economic Justice

Reviving the Love for Economic Justice

Foul Was Never Fair

Roshnee Ossewaarde-Lowtoo

LEXINGTON BOOKS
Lanham • Boulder • New York • London

Published by Lexington Books
An imprint of The Rowman & Littlefield Publishing Group, Inc.
4501 Forbes Boulevard, Suite 200, Lanham, Maryland 20706
www.rowman.com

86-90 Paul Street, London EC2A 4NE

British Library Cataloguing in Publication Information Available

Library of Congress Cataloging-in-Publication Data available

ISBN 9781793642103 (cloth) | ISBN 9781793642110 (epub)

Contents

Acknowledgments

Trust is the precondition for all human relationships and for all human endeavors. It is therefore one of the themes addressed in the present book. It has also played an important role at the beginning of, and throughout, the research that has resulted in the present work. I am greatly indebted to Paul van Geest who approached me six years ago to become part of the triad *Ad Fontes*, one of the projects that would be fully funded by the Goldschmeding Foundation. During a preliminary conversation, we explored the possible lines of my research and after an hour or so we agreed that trust, love, and power would be the major themes of my book. From that time onwards I was completely free to carry out my research. I am truly grateful for this trust and academic freedom. This also means that the views and commitments expressed in the present book do not necessarily reflect those of the Goldschmeding Foundation and of the Tilburg School of Catholic Theology, where my research took place. The other member of our small team, Joost Hengstmengel, must be mentioned here. I think back with joy on our regular conversations, emails and WhatsApp messages, and our symposium on the self-understandings that inform various conceptions of the economy.

The Goldschmeding Foundation is, of course, run by people, who are members of the Board, the Board of Trustees, the Supervisory Board, secretaries, financial officers, support staff, and so on. Though I am indebted to all of them, I am afraid that I cannot mention all names without omission. I will therefore confine myself to thanking the former members of the Board, Piero Overmars, Michiel de Wilde, and Jaap Winter, who had faith in the project *Ad Fontes*. I would also like to express my appreciation to the former communications managers, Dietske Bedeaux and Marijn van der Pas, for helping us disseminate our research. My thanks are also due to Wim Janse, who appeared on the scene as a supervisor a little more than a year after the project had started. He proved to be a good mediator and, perhaps just as importantly, a calm and calming presence.

A great part of my research took place at the Tilburg School of Catholic Theology, which provided me with the necessary physical amenities, intellectual boost, and moral support. I wish to thank my colleagues, including nonacademic staff, for their support as well as for the many conversations and laughs, especially during our lunch breaks and other informal meetings. My special thanks are due to Ada van der Velden-Westervelt, the managing director of the School, who played an important, mediating role on several occasions.

My first contact with Lexington Books/Rowman & Littlefield was the very competent and enthusiastic Michael (Mike) Gibson, who was assisted by Mikayla Mislak. Mike was succeeded by Trevor F. Crowell who proved to be just as dedicated, capable, and supportive. Both Mike and Trevor have been wonderful editors to work with. It goes without saying that I am deeply indebted to the anonymous reviewer for his/her feedback on an earlier draft of the present work.

Many have been a source of inspiration through their choices and ways of life, which often meant taking risks and giving up comfort and security for the sake of a higher good. In this regard, I would like to mention Amie Nagano, a dear friend of mine, who has turned her vision of a sustainable world into action by putting the ecological wisdom of ancient Japanese traditions into practice. Finally, I wish to express my gratitude to my family and friends for tolerating my seclusion during the past few years and to my husband Ringo for being my usual sounding board.

Introduction

In a fairer world than ours today, there would be democratic peoples that are peoples by virtue of their justice and civic friendship.[1] Such was Jacques Maritain's humanist conception of political society, whose roots can be traced back to ancient Greek and Roman political philosophy. The major difference between ancient philosophical traditions and modern democratic philosophies lies in the latter's universalization of the ancient "human dignity" and "citizenship." Christianity is usually deemed to have played a role in such universalization.[2] Historically, however, it took centuries for the idea of the equal "value" of every human being to manifest itself politically and socially. Modern political communities no longer rest on the institution of slavery and the idea that women are essentially unfit for citizenship, at least in theory. Conversely, modern economies are not perceived as the domain of noncitizens, namely, of slaves and lesser versions of males. Citizenship is the privilege and right of all those humans capable and willing to carry the political burden of fostering justice and civic friendship, which are "the essential foundations of that community of human persons which is political society."[3] Moderns are therefore expected to be both citizens and economic actors. This dual role of citizen and economic actor is highly challenging. It can lead to confusion about the relation between society and economy, both at the personal and collective levels. The exigencies of practical life may cause us to neglect our civic duties, especially the duty of cultivating our citizenship. They may also make us forget to raise the perennial questions regarding the conceivable goals of human life, the ends of society and the economy.

Notwithstanding the differences between ancient and modern political philosophies, the ancient wisdom that our economic activities are meant to serve the common good of all and everyone is still valid. Our labor and work become meaningful because of the higher good that they serve. Of course, the fact that justice and civic friendship constitute the foundation of our societies (in that imaginary, fairer world) means that labor and work are prevented from becoming soul-destroying and dehumanizing. The commitment to the common good of political communities, to justice, and civic friendship implies that these ideal democratic societies determine the form, content, and size of their economies and govern them. They ensure that private parties, such as private individuals and businesses, always act in accordance with the democratic values that sustain political communities and that transgressions are punished. This means that they also prevent great inequalities and ensure that the wealthy do not have a disproportionate influence on political decision-making and hence on whole societies. In other words, economies are thoroughly embedded in societies and are thus governed by the very same values constituting these democratic societies. People living in such societies do not live their lives as Jekyll and Hyde. Instead, they are able to reconcile utility and self-regard, on the one hand, with justice and the common good, on the other. Such reconciliation may demand sacrifices and self-denial. Yet, such transcendence of self-interest is far from being heroic. It is quite common among those who truly care for each other and are thus willing to carry the burdens of each other.

FACING OUR UNDEMOCRATIC REALITIES

The ideal commonwealth as imagined above has never been and most probably will never be. It is nonetheless still remarkable that the aspiration to such a humane order has become so weak. Present economic arrangements are characterized by a high degree of laissez-faireism or, in any case, a steadfast faith in "markets," asymmetric economic power relations and inequalities, starvation wages for many and exorbitant incomes for the few, overproduction, overconsumption, and overinvestment in technological development, the multiplication of wants, and the cultivation of greed and envy.[4] So-called division of labor and specialization have not only led to monotonous and soul-destroying work, uprooting through the demand of mobility, but even more fundamentally, to the division between "manual" and "mental" labor (whereby "mental" is not necessarily "intellectual" since clerical work, data entry, data mining, and so many other "white-collar" jobs do not require full intellectual effort). These divisions do not only alienate us from each other, but also from ourselves. They undermine the creation of wholesome individualities, personalities, or selves.[5] The contrast between our economic lives and the democratic ideal could not be starker. In some sense, we might be worse off than our ancient counterparts because the line between servitude and freedom has become blurry.[6] As Hannah Arendt remarks, "man cannot be free if he does not know that he is subject to necessity, because his freedom is always won in his never wholly successful attempts to liberate himself from necessity."[7] Most of us are primarily and solely economic subjects—and hence subject to (economic) necessity—and never get to be citizens (and hence free).

Our economic "necessity," however, is no *natural* necessity. It is a necessity imposed by a societal apparatus informed by the logic of domination and exploitation, which stems from the conceptual objectification of the world.[8] The "struggle for existence," a terminology that was coined during the so-called Industrial Revolution, characterizes this societal apparatus.[9] The "productive apparatus," Herbert Marcuse writes, "perpetuates the struggle for existence and extends it to a total international struggle which ruins the lives of those who build and use this apparatus."[10] The ideals and values that constitute a social body seem quasi-inexistent in what Pierre Bourdieu refers to as the "economic field," which is mostly experienced as a battlefield in which the economic agent is involved "in an 'indirect conflict' with all those engaged in the same game."[11] We are able (and perhaps, compelled) to split ourselves into calculating economic actors in the economic sphere and loving friends and parents in the private sphere. That said, even in our private homes, we are not protected from the frenzy of competitive life. We are groomed for success and inculcated with the idea that we must surpass others. This emphasis on achievement, superiority, and domination, which is meta-economic or pre-economic, takes economic forms in the context of economism. This non-economic dimension of economism is overlooked when we concentrate our anger and outrage on "markets," "capitalism," or the "bad guys." We thereby misconstrue the nature of the problem, underestimate its magnitude and the cultural revolution required for more humane living conditions.

Why have we given up the mission of "civilization and culture," which, for Maritain, is the political task par excellence?[12] Perhaps even more importantly for the present purpose, what is required to take it up again? My claim that we have indeed given up the political task of humanization is reflected in the inversion of the relationship between politics and the economy. The end of society has come to be conceived largely in economic terms. Correspondingly, the end of politics has also been degraded to the subsidiary role of supporting an economic society.[13] The subordination of political power to economic forces often means that governments have their hands tied. Corporate blackmail and the threat of capital flight, with the corresponding fear of unemployment, can render governments quite powerless. Yet, private economic forces have not taken over whole economies and hence societies overnight. Neither necessity nor invisible forces got us where we are today, as both Karl Polanyi and Susan Strange already pointed out, decades ago.[14] At decisive points in history, political decisions, motivated by ideals contrary to justice and civic friendship, have contributed to the "emancipation" of "the economy" from democratic control. Such "emancipation," I will be arguing, has been enabled because of the disintegration or absence of a substantive social bond constituted by civic friendship and justice.

In other words, economic institutions and practices that undermine democratic values and foster socioeconomic injustice cannot only be blamed on economic theories or flawed economic models. These flawed theories and models are cultural products, the cumulative consequences of ideas, beliefs, and practices that arose in particular historical contexts. These ideas, beliefs, and practices have somehow succeeded in dismantling the social fabric, impeding and undermining the democratic project of universal justice and fraternity. "Fraternity" is here used as a gender-neutral noun. Though "solidarity" is an even more gender-neutral term, it is not the exact equivalent of fraternity, fellowship, or civic friendship. An enquiry into their different etymologies, cultural contexts, and underpinning ontologies would require a separate work. For the time being, let me suggest two differences. One is that "fraternity" is more metaphysically loaded, while "solidarity" tends to evoke the unity between individuals without alluding to any *essential* bond between fellow beings. It could thus be said that the idea of fraternity precedes concrete solidarities. The second subtle difference can perhaps best be understood as the difference between friendship between equals and "friendship" between unequals. The solidarity of the rich *with* the poor is not a reciprocal friendship and is moreover apolitical. It can thus also happen in undemocratic contexts.

Civic friendship, on the other hand, presumes political equality. The question of whether such political equality (and equal political participation) is possible when the socioeconomic conditions of citizens are marked by great inequalities is one that I cannot address comprehensively.[15] However, as the reader may have noticed, I do mention these inequalities above and consider them as undemocratic and as undermining the democratic project. As I will argue in later chapters, if we are truly committed to the democratic project, then we must re-appraise our hierarchy of values or statuses that we attribute to various activities and adjust our wages accordingly. Such critical revaluation requires that we be constantly aware of the persistent influence of our inherited contempt or disregard for the body on our judgements and institutions. The modern democratic commitment also requires a more equal redistribution of physical burdens, stultifying activities, and intellectual activities. We cannot possibly want to repeat the ancient division between slaves and women, on the one hand, and citizens, on the other hand. In his *Tyranny of Merits* (2020), Michael J. Sandel considers some kind of equality of condition as the precondition for democratic life. Instead of equality of opportunity or results, he proposes "a broad equality of condition that enables those who do not achieve great wealth or prestigious positions to live lives of decency and dignity."[16]

Great inequalities segregate people and prevent them from sharing a common, democratic life. In *The Revolt of the Elites and the Betrayal of Democracy* (1995), Christopher Lasch articulates a similar argument, noting that "social and civic equality presuppose at least a rough approximation of economic equality."[17] Both Lasch and Sandel blame political elites for the failure of democracies. They thereby express the insight that bad leadership is contagious and affects whole societies. Even more fundamentally, the predominance of technocratic politics has overshadowed the indispensability of virtues in politics. Of course, failed and unvirtuous leadership does not arise in a vacuum but is both a symptom and consequence of a general cultural malaise. This also means that so-called ordinary people are not simply victims. The victimization of "the people," that is, the manipulation of our feelings in order to make us feel that we are victims of the elite is an important weapon of demagogues. It is noteworthy that Cicero emphasizes the "depraved opinions of men" when dealing with the bad leadership that led to the collapse of the Republic.[18] These "depraved opinions" are ideas about the ends of human life and of societies, about the measures of success and failure, and so on. In other words, depraved opinions are those prevailing ideas and beliefs in a given cultural context that undermine civic friendship and justice.

A PHENOMENOLOGY OF OUR ECONOMIC LIVES

The main argument of the present work, therefore, is that the focus on "the economy" must be enlarged to encompass the culture underpinning it. In previous centuries, it was quite common for social critics, some philosophers, economists, and psychoanalysts to consider their lived economic realities as part of their cultural contexts and to reflect on them as such. Today such comprehensive approach to our economic issues is much less frequent, largely because of disciplinary specialization. The present work tries to fill up this lacuna and transcend prevailing disciplinary boundaries, while drawing on these very disciplines. This multidisciplinary and "cultural" approach is partly inspired by Charles Taylor's comprehensive approach to the big questions. "Culture" is here accordingly conceived as the "constellation of understandings of person, nature, society, and the good."[19] The twofold main question that I raised above, namely, why have we given up the democratic task of humanization and how can we take it up again can thus be further specified as a question regarding our possibilities to overcome those features of our culture that make it more difficult for us to make justice and civic friendship our priorities at the personal and collective levels.

What the present book does not try to be is yet another critique of capitalism as such or an advocacy of socialism or communism as an alternative. This tendency to restrict our possibilities a priori to these two historical possibilities is hardly helpful and only serves to reinforce the status quo. Margaret Stout, for example, refers to a third historical alternative, besides capitalism and communism, which consists in a political economy based on "equitably meeting human needs, association through the social bond, intersubjective understanding, and mutuality."[20] Alternatives require a different self-understanding and a different way of relating to the world. Despite their different ideologies, the historical forms of capitalism, socialism, and communism are undergirded by a very similar vision of the world and self-understanding, which has been causing so much havoc. We have become habituated to seeing ourselves as masters of the universe and have accordingly granted ourselves the illegitimate right to subject the world (or nature) to our will.[21] Such practical anthropomorphism, as Gabriel Marcel calls it, follows from our weak sense of awe.[22] Or, as Iris Murdoch puts it, we have too grand a picture of ourselves in which "we have isolated, and identified ourselves with, an unrealistic conception of will."[23] The humanization of our economic life will therefore require our discarding the pictures that are preventing us from imagining and seeing alternatives.[24] It will also require courage to live out these alternatives.

The reader might wonder whom "we" refers to in this book. In her commendable *The Economics of Enough: How to Run the Economy as if the Future Matters* (2011), Diane Coyle defines that "we" as the "majority of people in rich Western societies [who] have been consuming 'too much,' according to the evidence from the scale of the increase in the amount of carbon dioxide in the atmosphere, and the likely increase in the Earth's surface temperature."[25] It can hardly be denied that rich countries have become wealthy by appropriating communal property or what has come to be referred to as "the commons." In these countries, the consumption of natural resources is up to tenfold that of poorer countries.[26] Yet, it is to be expected that developing countries will catch up with the richer countries since they too want the same level of material welfare that their richer counterparts have been enjoying for much longer. "We" therefore must be much more inclusive and encompass all nations or civilizations, rich and poor, that are in thrall to the mainstream idea of progress. That said, it is incumbent on richer or more "developed" countries to accept the greater burdens of the transformations required for economic and social justice for all today and for future generations since the former have been the front-runners to the abyss.[27]

Hence, though the ideas and images that I will be discussing are characteristic of "Western culture," the propositions to overcome the obstacles to civic friendship and justice may also be valid in other cultural contexts.[28]

Prevailing economic arrangements, including the subordination of politics to economics, are not peculiar to the West. Conversely, different ways of thinking and living that have arisen in "non-Western" cultural contexts can help us articulate alternatives for our specific Western contexts.[29] These alternatives may require that we learn new attitudes toward the world and ourselves. Degrowth and postgrowth proposals from various disciplinary perspectives, "critical green growth," more integral and richer conceptions of development, "progress," or "prosperity" abound.[30] Individuals and communities have taken up lifestyles that negate the limits of the materialist conception of human life. They are those whom Ernst Friedrich Schumacher called "home-comers," that is, those "people in search of a new life-style, who seek to return to certain basic truths about man and his world."[31] Yet, these movements and communities are minorities and are constantly under threat, especially in those parts of the world where laws are absent or ineffective, and where sheer force and impunity thus rule.[32] Modern imagination seems unable to envision a paradigm that does not have economic growth as its highest goal.[33] We are so captivated by the idea that only economic growth can guarantee employment, peace, and security, and keep people contented—make us "happy"—that we are unwilling and incapable of re-imagining human life whose overriding and sole concern is no longer economic welfare. So, what can help us unlearn the *après nous, le déluge* attitude and make us more sensitive to the needs of those unrelated to us and of those yet to be born? What can make us *love* justice?

My emphasis on the "love" for justice reflects both my philosophical commitment and the corresponding belief that the best institutions or constitutions for that matter are not self-sustaining, but are instead dependent on people's devotion to them. The term "devotion" captures the quite self-evident idea that such commitment is not only a matter of cognitive conviction. Just institutions and laws demand our undivided and steadfast love to be effective. In a slightly different terminology, we cannot have just laws and institutions without virtuous citizens who, by reason of their virtues, are able to sustain these laws and institutions. These "virtues," however, must be purified of their androcentric connotation, and in fact, they are "devirilized" when love is conceived as a prerequisite for justice.[34] The ancient and modern rationalist emphasis on the intellect as the source of virtue is thereby corrected. "Love" will be further qualified since it is an unwavering and lucid love and thus neither the capricious love of Cupid nor the blind love of fanatics. My philosophical commitment is thus phenomenological, broadly construed. Such a philosophy begins with human experience and existence in full awareness that phenomenology and ontology are intricately related and can correct each other. As Taylor puts it, the challenge is "how to align our best phenomenology with an adequate ontology, how to resolve a seeming lack of fit [. . .] either by enriching one's ontology or by revising or challenging the phenomenology."[35] Given the extraordinary task of humanization that lies before us, I do not deem it sensible to restrict a priori either our ontology or our phenomenology to the limits of modern naturalisms. Therefore, I am sympathetic to Maritain's integral humanism and other forms of humanism that integrate ancient, modern, and religious intuitions about the heights of the good and the depths of evil.

FROM DOMINANCE TO REVERENCE

In chapter 1, I will be looking at the particular visions of the world and self-understandings that have suppressed—and are still suppressing—the ideal of humanization. Of course, certain practices correspond to these ideas, beliefs, and images even if the latter are fictive. A flawed image can become real enough through its collective endorsement. Hence, though the image of an invulnerable and self-sufficient being is more fictive than real, we may want to live up to that image because it is simply part of our social imaginary. In doing so we become not so much invulnerable as insensitive and indifferent to the plight of those around us. I will outline an alternative self-understanding that results in a political economy whose aim is the fulfilment of the genuine needs of all. This is also when justice prevails. I thereby neither pretend nor try to identify and determine these "genuine needs." The main premise of that alternative self-understanding is that we are all *essentially* related to each other and therefore responsible for each other. Such an understanding of human existence and fellowship is metaphysical, religious, mystical or poetic. Yet, as I will argue, one need not be metaphysically or religiously inclined to imagine such an alternative political economy. Stout's conceived "political economy of love and abundance" simply presumes such an alternative ontology.[36] The economists Luigino Bruni and Anouk Grevin defend an economy of communion.[37] Similarly, for Hendrik Opdebeeck, an "economy of communion" arises when the philosophy of responsibility is integrated into economic thinking and practices.[38] That said, given the philosophical nature of the present work, I cannot ignore the vexing question of ontology. In the next pages, I thus explain why I deem it necessary to "translate" certain ideas that are associated with particular religious traditions into a more common language. This "common" language, however, cannot be the dominant language of naturalistic materialism.

The conception of the economy as an economy of communion rests on the idea that the economy serves the higher goal of human communion or fellowship. In fact, as I argue in chapter 2, it presupposes that love is the telos—both the highest goal and moving force—of human existence. Since the idea that the "law of love" ought to inform our standards of justice is a Judaic and Christian notion, even if not exclusively so, I briefly revisit Augustine's legacy of that idea, examine Reinhold Niebuhr's updated (and modified) version of that legacy and the alternative represented by Martin Buber's dialogic love. There has been much written on different conceptions of love, including *agape*, and I therefore do not wish to repeat these studies in this book.[39] Such a discussion would be an unnecessary digression from the main objectives of the present work. I thus confine myself to further qualifying the love that could possibly support a highly demanding form of justice by concentrating on the aforementioned thinkers. Since I consider these ideas of love and justice to be on par with comparable or rival ideas from so-called secular philosophical traditions, I believe that the ideal of love—even if it has religious sources—can resonate with those of us who are not committed to these specific religious traditions. Of course, the previous reasoning requires that we transcend the dichotomy between "reason" and "revelation" so that both religious and so-called "secular" ideas can be critically and philosophically appraised. Even more pertinently perhaps, "reason" must be redefined as the thinking of beings who are bodies, spirits, and more. It is a thinking informed by the unreserved engagement with the world, our deepest commitments, including the commitment to truth and poetic imagination. The ideal of love, Niebuhr observes, is not "superimposed upon human history by scriptural, or any other, authority. Human existence, when profoundly analyzed, yields the law of love as the final law of human freedom."[40] The law of love has long been conceived as irrelevant to politics and matters of social justice. In Niebuhr's thought, it regains its full significance, becoming the "impossible possibility," the ultimate and critical perspective from which prevailing forms of justice and philanthropy are judged. Love is also the power that sustains our striving for justice. Buber fittingly dubs it the "motive power of the infinite." Buber's recourse to dialogue, I hold, is an attempt to rescue the metaphysical dimension of love, while liberating the latter from many theological obscurities.

The dialogical way of life is an end and vocation rather than a pregiven fact. Real life is far removed from this ideal. An important obstacle to mutuality is our own selves, and more precisely, nonunified selves. The care of the self is therefore an important part of the present book and is dealt with in chapter 3. Justice begins with oneself and, in the very first place, with a healthy personhood. Such wholeness of the self, I argue, is the precondition for socioeconomic justice, for humane and humanizing workplaces and economies. The idea of the unity of the self or of the soul is a central idea in Plato's *Politeia* (*The Republic*) and in Jewish and Christian thought. To be just is to be just with one's whole being, throughout one's whole life and not simply in a particular context and with respect to a particular act. The chapter begins with a critical re-appraisal of the concept "self-love." The argument is that the emphasis on too much self-love clouds the real issues. "Narcissism" and "egoism" (terms that I will further qualify) are the real problems, but they precisely follow from too much negligence of the self. The care of the self takes place in fellowship with others and through the care for others. As Abraham Heschel writes, "man achieves fullness of being in fellowship, in care for others. He expands his existence by 'bearing his fellow-man's burden'."[41] Such care for others consists not only in sympathy but also in practices. This emphasis on our physical involvement is not superfluous since both "caring" and "self" tend to have psychical connotations. I argue that the integration of caring activities into our daily life, especially if the latter involves predominantly "mental operations performed in an office," can help us counter our alienation from common life and life itself.[42] Since the transcendence of the fragmentation of the self partly depends on an active conscience, I will also consider ways in which we can re-activate a dormant conscience. To this end, I largely draw on Rousseau's writings on this theme.

The idiom "change begins with oneself" is only partly true. Our struggle to be whole and hence to be just can be severely undermined by features of our culture that we have simply inherited and thus take for granted. In chapter 4, I argue that the cultural preference for utility and expediency over justice saps our personal love for justice. It would perhaps be more accurate to speak in terms of the *bourgeois* preference for utility and expediency, following Art Carden's and Deirdre McCloskey's claim that we live in the "Bourgeois Era."[43] Conceptually, the preference for utility and expediency over justice is captured by the expression "fair is foul, and foul is fair." This phrase appears in the first scene of Act I of Shakespeare's Macbeth. It is precisely in the sense meant by Shakespeare that Keynes uses the expression in his talk (and later, essay) *Economic Possibilities for Our Grandchildren* (1928). Keynes saw that economic growth throve on vices, but he also perceived growth to be necessary to end poverty. He therefore deplored the fact that we had to give up traditional morality but saw this as a necessary evil for a greater good. He believed that once we satisfied our needs, we would stop pretending that evil is good and simply go back to the truth. For the time being, we must keep up the pretense.[44] Practically, the cultural and political prioritization of utility and expediency has manifested itself in attempts to create "market societies," which in fact entailed abandoning the ideal of communion. The reversal of traditional morality has resulted in the neutralization of what used to be conceived as vices, but also in the erasure of the line demarcating needs from wants. Consequently, the passion for comfort and wealth has become paramount, and the slope toward human insatiability has been freed from obstacles. Such a condition, I maintain, is dehumanizing and contrary to the democratic project. I therefore propose the re-introduction of the distinction between limited needs and unlimited wants (desires). I also show that the bourgeois ideology that economies should be ruled by markets and that the latter should be as "free" as possible guarantees injustice. If we still aspire to be genuine democratic communities, then markets must be subordinated to the democratic ideals of justice and civic friendship.

Particular self-understandings and visions of the world are better able to support the love for justice than others. A separative model of human nature is the least appropriate to that task. Similarly, the world conceived as indifferent or as chaos is the least likely to gain our allegiance. Our love for justice is weakened when we face a world of chaos, both conceptually and practically. Responsibility can only be accepted for a world that does not reward injustice and for people to whom we somehow feel related. We have grown accustomed to the image of the world as being "absurd," devoid of sense, value, or wisdom. Such a world can be used and exploited but cannot be loved or revered. This also holds for all the beings that make it up. In chapter 5, I develop the idea that in order to counter this instrumental attitude toward the world, we need to regain our capacity for awe and reverence, and this, of course, requires a less alienating self-understanding.[45] Such an attitude of awe and reverence can counter what I refer to as "existential mistrust." In *Thinking Nature: An Essay in Negative Ecology* (2019), Sean McGrath convincingly defends the idea that reverence and contemplation are necessary complements to environmental activism and powerful counterweights to what he calls "eco-anxiety."[46] This existential attitude of awe and reverence is what the ancients referred to as "piety," and Niebuhr calls "primary religion."[47] Piety is admittedly demanded toward family and homeland, but it can be extended to the whole humankind and the world, a tendency that can be discerned in Stoic thought. As far as "primary religion" is concerned, it precedes established religions. It is neither some kind of "common core" in all religions nor a form of "civil religion." Piety or a primary religion can arguably help us transcend the pessimism (bordering on misanthropy), fear, denial, and the shallow optimism that plague debates about the ecological crisis. An attitude of awe and reverence, I hold, can be fostered by the humanization of our immediate living environments, including our working environment. I therefore emphasize the political and corporate responsibility to provide and stimulate environments that inspire trust and a genuine concern for others.

NOTES

1. Jacques Maritain, *Christianity and Democracy and the Rights of Man and Natural Law*, trans. Doris C. Anson (San Francisco: Ignatius Press, 1986), 121.

2. Maritain thus writes: "The consciousness of the dignity of the person and of the rights of the person remained implicit in pagan antiquity, over which the law of slavery cast its shadow. It was the message of the Gospel which suddenly awakened this consciousness, in a divine and transcendent form, revealing to men that they are called upon to be the sons and heirs of God in the kingdom of God." Ibid, 147.

3. Ibid, 121.

4. For the close connection between capitalism, science, and technics in the West, see the first chapter of Lewis Mumford, *Technics and Civilization* (New York and Burlingame: Harcourt, Brace & World, Inc., 1963).

5. A classic work on this theme is Herbert Marcuse, *One-Dimensional Man: Studies in the Ideology of Advanced Industrial Society* (London and New York: Routledge, 1964).

6. This modern servitude is quite vividly described by Mumford: "In short, the machine came into our civilization, not to save man from the servitude to ignoble forms of work, but to make more widely possible the servitude to ignoble standards of consumption that had grown up among the military aristocracies." Mumford, *Technics and Civilization*, 105–106.

7. Hannah Arendt, *The Human Condition* (Chicago and London: The University of Chicago Press, 1958), 121.

8. Marcuse, *One-Dimensional Man*, 128.

9. Mumford, *Technics and Civilization*, 187.

10. Marcuse, *One-Dimensional Man*, 148.

11. Pierre Bourdieu, *The Social Structures of the Economy*, trans. Chris Turner (Cambridge/Malden, MA: Polity, 2008), 199, 208.

12. Maritain, *Christianity and Democracy*, 57.

13. This situation has been repeatedly criticized by Michael J. Sandel in his various works, including in his recent book *The Tyranny of Merit: What's Become of the Common Good?* (New York: Farrar, Straus and Giroux, 2020).

14. Susan Strange, *Casino Capitalism* (Oxford: Basil Blackwell, 1986), 63; Karl Polanyi, *The Great Transformation: The Political and Economic Origins of Our Time* (Boston: Beacon Press, 2001). Marcuse, similarly, writes: "The way in which a society organizes the life of its members involves an initial *choice* between historical alternatives which are determined by the inherited level of the material and intellectual culture. The choice itself results from the play of the dominant interests. It *anticipates* specific modes of transforming and utilizing man and nature and rejects other modes. It is one 'project' of realization among others." Marcuse, *One-Dimensional Man*, xlvi.

15. I would like to refer the reader to Cicero's discussion of this theme in the first book of *De Re Publica*. Marcus Tullius Cicero, "On the Republic," in *On the Republic and On the Laws*, trans. David Fott (Ithaca: Cornell University Press, 2014).

16. Sandel, *The Tyranny of Merit*, 224.

17. Christopher Lasch, *The Revolt of the Elites and the Betrayal of Democracy* (New York and London: W.W. Norton & Company, 1995), 22.

18. Cicero, "On the Republic," 52 (Book I, 51–52).

19. Charles Taylor, "Modernity and the Rise of the Public Sphere," in *The Tanner Lectures on Human Values*, ed. Grethe B. Peterson (Salt Lake City: University of Utah Press, 1993), 213.

20. Margaret Stout, "Back to the Future: Toward a Political Economy of Love and Abundance," *Administration and Society* 42, no. 1 (2010): 3–37, 9.

21. And this is the reason why we need a new metaphysics of nature, as Sean McGrath rightly points out. See Sean J. McGrath, *Thinking Nature: An Essay in Negative Ecology* (Edinburgh: Edinburgh University Press, 2019).

22. Gabriel Marcel, *The Decline of Wisdom* (New York: Philosophical Library, 1955), 42.

23. Iris Murdoch, *The Sovereignty of Good* (New York: Schocken Books, 1971), 47.

24. This notion of being "captured by a picture" is expounded by Charles Taylor in *A Secular Age* (Cambridge MA: The Belknap Press of Harvard University Press, 2007), 549, 551.

25. Diane Coyle, *The Economics of Enough: How to Run the Economy as if the Future Matters* (Princeton and Oxford: Princeton University Press, 2011), 76.

26. Stefan Giljum et al., "Overconsumption: Our Use of the World's Natural Resources," Friends of the Earth International (September 3, 2009), accessed April 30, 2021, https://www.foei.org/resources/publications/publications-by-subject/economic-justice-resisting-neoliberalism-publications/overconsumption-our-use-of-the-worlds-natural-resources.

27. Cf. Nicholas Stern: "The rich countries have special responsibility for where the world is now, and thus for the consequences which flow from this difficult starting point, whereas poor countries will be particularly badly hit." Nicholas Stern, *The Economics of Climate Change: The Stern Review* (Cambridge: Cambridge University Press, 2007), 33.

28. I am aware of the fact that the terminology "Western culture" or the "West" is far too much of a generalization given the cultural diversity among so-called Western countries. Readers from different countries might conclude that the tensions between different values and ideals have been addressed in different ways in their own cultural contexts.

29. These alternatives are, for instance, articulated in Gustavo Esteva and Madhu Suri Prakash, *Grassroots Postmodernism: Remaking the Soil of Cultures* (London: Zed Books, 2014).

30. See, for example, Stout, "Back to the Future"; Diego Vazquez-Brust, Alastair M. Smith, and Joseph Sarkis, "Managing the Transition to Critical Green Growth: The 'Green Growth State'," *Futures* 64 (2014): 38–50; Vincent Liegey and Anitra Nelson, *Exploring Degrowth: A Critical Guide* (London: Pluto Press, 2020).

31. Ernst Friedrich Schumacher, *Small is Beautiful: A Study of Economics as if People Mattered* (London: Blond & Briggs, 1976), 144.

32. Kate Hallam, "Environmental Defenders: Murdered, Missing and At Risk," *Socialist Lawyer* 75 (2017), 40–43, https://doi.org/10.13169/socialistlawyer.75.0040; Jonathan Watts and John Vidal, "Environmental Defenders Being Killed in Record Numbers Globally, New Research Reveals," *Chain Reaction* 130, September 2017, 40.

33. See Ekaterina Chertkovskaya, Alexander Paulsson, and Stefania Barca (eds.), *Towards a Political Economy of Degrowth* (London: Rowman & Littlefield International, 2019). In their introduction to the edited collection of contributions, the editors point out the hegemony of the growth paradigm and the political struggle for a degrowth counterhegemony.

34. For a brief account of the close connection between male virility and virtue and between androcentrism and domination, see Pierre Bourdieu, *Masculine Domination*, trans. Richard Nice (Stanford, CA: Stanford University Press, 2001), 12, 52.

35. Taylor, *A Secular Age*, 609.

36. Stout, "Back to the Future," 9.

37. Luigino Bruni and Anouk Grevin, *L'économie Silencieuse* (Bruyères-le-Châtel: Nouvelle Cité, 2016).

38. Hendrik Opdebeeck, *The Economy and Meaningfulness: A Utopia?* (Brussels: Peter Lang, 2019), 130.

39. An excellent work on this subject is Catherine Osborne, *Eros Unveiled: Plato and the God of Love* (Oxford: Clarendon Press, 2002). The various contributions in Craig A. Boyd, ed., *Visions of Agapé: Problems and Possibilities in Human and Divine Love* (Hampshire: Ashgate, 2008) similarly help to correct tenacious dichotomies.

40. Reinhold Niebuhr, *Faith and Politics: A Commentary on Religious, Social and Political Thought in a Technological Age*, ed. Ronald H. Stone (New York: George Braziller, 1968), 145.

41. Abraham J. Heschel, *Who is Man?* (Stanford, CA: Stanford University Press, 1965), 47.

42. Lasch, *The Revolt of the Elites and the Betrayal of Democracy*, 20.

43. Art Carden and Deirdre Nansen McCloskey, "The Bourgeois Deal: Leave Me Alone, and I'll Make You Rich," *SSRN,* March 8, 2018, 41–42, https://dx.doi.org/10.2139/ssrn.3155530.

44. Keynes, "Economic Possibilities for Our Grandchildren," 331.

45. Cf. Heschel, *Who is Man?*, 89.

46. McGrath, *Thinking Nature*, 141.

47. Reinhold Niebuhr, *Christianity and Power Politics* (Hamden, CT: Archon Books, 1969), 178.

Chapter 1

From the Struggle for Existence to Communion

THE NONECONOMIC ROOTS OF ECONOMISM

What John Maynard Keynes and Susan Strange dubbed a "casino capitalism," and Robert and Edward Skidelsky refer to as "Darwinian capitalism" could only arise and take root because the ground was already prepared for it.[1] A culture was ready to receive it. And this same culture is still sustaining inhumane and ecologically disastrous economic practices. Of course, once particular power structures are established, they are not easily changed however much our self-understanding or attitude to the world might change. But clearly, these power structures are maintained because there is no strong motive for radical change. In other words, even if we choose to focus on power relations to explain our condition, the question of why the motives of power and gain are stronger than those of fellowship and justice remains. At the outset, I have argued that in order to understand the idea and reality of an autonomous economic sphere in which baser passions are legitimate, we must look at the noneconomic beliefs, ideas, and practices that undermine fraternity and justice and legitimize baser passions—such as ordinary greed, vanity, and the desire for profit and power. The argument in this section is that such a perversion of economic life is the unintended consequence of a long tradition of reform and disciplining that has often involved the alliance between religious and secular (in the sense of "worldly") powers.[2] These cultural transformations have entailed a changed self-understanding, resulting in a "disengaged" and instrumental attitude to a world conceived as "neutral," our bodies, and even to our "minds" and "selves," similarly considered to be objectifiable.

The background to our present economic condition can be traced back to the Late Middle Ages. This is the period of great reforms both at the religious and societal levels, or the early beginnings of what Taylor calls the "disciplinary society," in agreement with Michel Foucault.[3] This is thus when, according to Mumford, an isolation and intensification of the "power motive" becomes visible. He writes:

> Each element in life forms part of a cultural mesh: one part implicates, restrains, helps to express the other. During this period the mesh was broken, and a fragment escaped and launched itself on a separate career—the will to dominate the environment. To dominate, not to cultivate; to seize power, not to achieve form.[4]

Similarly, Polanyi interprets the collapse of the medieval economy in terms of a disruption of an equilibrium between motives. According to him,

> All economic systems known to us up to the end of feudalism in Western Europe were organized either on the principle of reciprocity or redistribution, or householding, or some combination of the three. [. . .] In this framework, the orderly production and distribution of goods was secured through a variety of individual motives disciplined by general principles of behavior. Among these motives gain was not prominent.[5]

The pregnant questions that hereby arise concern the reasons why the cultural mesh broke down, and how, as a result, the motives of gain and power became so dominant. Mumford indicates two possible explanations. One of them, of course, is the change in the conception of space and time between the fourteenth and seventeenth century, as the idea of a cosmic order faded away. As a result, time became homogeneous and linear, and "space as hierarchy of values was replaced by space as a system of magnitudes."[6]

A new economic mentality corresponded to the shift from the symbolic understanding of nature and the world to the mechanistic understanding of nature and the world. The propensity to *calculate* individual gain, which was previously thwarted by the primacy of social relations and obligations, now became legitimate.[7] A remarkable aspect of this preoccupation with profit is its monetary and hence abstract character. As Mumford notes:

> Men became powerful to the extent that they neglected the real world of wheat and wool, food and clothes, and centered their attention on the purely quantitative representation of it in tokens and symbols. [. . .] The power that was science and the power that was money were, in final analysis, the same kind of power: the power of abstraction, measurement, quantification.[8]

This calculating reason is a distinctive feature of what would become the modern "buffered self," to use Taylor's terminology. It requires "disengagement" not only from intimate social relationships but also from feelings, intuitions, and "certain bodily functions."[9] This disengagement and disembodiment, as I will be arguing, alienates people from the (real) world and their fellow beings. It makes it easier for them to exploit the natural environment and other beings.

The second possible explanation for the intensification of the will-to-power to which Mumford refers is worthy of note. He suggests that the will-to-power became stronger in response to a collectively experienced sense of inferiority. The latter arose from the great gap between the ideals of holiness and perfection, on the one hand, and the ugly reality of wars and enmities, depravity of church leaders, and the unredeemed misery of human existence, on the other hand.[10] Though it is quite difficult for us today to ascertain whether there was such a compensation going on, it is remarkable that there was what Taylor calls a "rage for order," which is hard to explain. As Taylor notes,

> What is peculiar to Latin Christendom is a growing concern with Reform, a drive to make over the whole society to higher standards. I don't pretend to have the explanation of this "rage for order," but it seems to me to be a fact about the late-mediaeval and early modern period, and moreover one which has carried over into the modern period in the partly secularized ideal of "civilization."[11]

Taylor points to the notable attempts to universalize a way of life that, for centuries, was mostly embraced by an "elite." The belief that all, and not only an elite, can and ought to strive for improvement or perfection can be considered as a derivative of Christianity's universalism. This belief, according to Taylor, informed later attempts to remake whole societies, till our age today. The alliance between religious and secular powers to the common end of a (Christian) civilization during the Renaissance contributes to an increasing emphasis on self-discipline and to a disciplinary society. Self-discipline and a high sexual ethic now become the norms for peasant communities too.

The Reformation, which Taylor considers to be the "radical Reform"—the culmination of the long tradition of Reform—brings about two important transformations that are relevant to the present purpose, namely, the desacralization of the world and the affirmation of ordinary, productive life.[12] I would like to add a third paradoxical development, which is a certain disregard for the human, also characteristic of capitalism and later "satanic mills."[13] It is paradoxical because the "affirmation of ordinary life" tends to evoke an affirmation of total life, including its bodiliness, pleasures, and pains. What I am calling a disregard for the human can best be understood as the integration of monastic asceticism and self-denial into the ordinary life of "lay people." Radical Protestantism, as Taylor notes, loads "ordinary flourishing with a burden of renunciation it cannot carry. It in fact fills out the picture of what the properly sanctified life would be with a severe set of moral demands."[14] Or, as Mumford puts it,

> Protestantism re-enforced these lessons of middle class sobriety and gave them God's sanction. True: the main devices of finance were a product of Catholic Europe, and Protestantism has received undeserved praise as a liberating force from medieval routine and undeserved censure as the original source and spiritual justification of modern capitalism. But the peculiar office of Protestantism was to unite finance to the concept of a godly life and to turn the asceticism countenanced by religion into a device for concentration upon worldly goods and worldly advancement. [. . .] In the last analysis, the individual must fend for himself in heaven, as he did on the exchange.[15]

By rejecting many common practices as idolatry, superstition, and idleness, and by stressing the sovereignty of God, Protestantism helped not only to remove any divine presence from the material world and hence to despiritualize the latter but also to destroy the bond that makes all humans responsible for each other. It therefore exacerbated an individualism already visible in Augustine's writings.

The affirmation of ordinary life can be understood negatively, in the sense of the delegitimization of any goal beyond productive and reproductive life, such as contemplation and spiritual transformation by participating in divine love. In the post-Reformation western world, this divinely sanctioned concentration on worldly goods and progress gradually becomes the highest conceivable human goal. Against the background of religious moralism, ongoing "religious" wars and intolerance, it is perhaps understandable that thinkers such as Grotius and Locke sought minimalist common grounds for a peaceful living together. What is more natural and rational—that is to say, in agreement with reason—than self-preservation and well-being? From these simple and undisputable principles follows an order of mutual respect and benefit, which is conducive to peace and prosperity. As Taylor writes:

> Gradually this normative order turns into a blueprint for the kind of society the reconstruction aims at. These rational, sociable beings, meant to live together in respect for each other's life and liberty, are also meant to preserve themselves by industrious exploitation of their natural surroundings. Properly carried out, this exploitation leads to economic growth. The right to property both follows immediately from this exploitation of nature, and also makes possible improvement and hence economic growth.[16]

Yet, this minimalist and "economistic" conceptualization of the ends of human life is not merely a response to irrational carnages and dogmatisms.

It is, perhaps in the first place, an affirmation of the self-understanding as sovereign selves or individuals who own themselves and whose highest goal ought to be human flourishing or happiness.

The personal motive of economic gain, which had been gaining ground since the Late Middle Ages, becomes a virtue in the seventeenth and eighteenth century since it is conducive to prosperity. The idea of society as an economic society that is peaceful precisely because all individuals pursue their economic self-interests becomes a desirable alternative to destructive military conquests. Voltaire, for instance, praised the *douces moeurs* of commercial society and admired the peaceful interaction among traders at the "respectable" London Stock Exchange.[17] More cynically or realistically (depending on one's view of human nature), Keynes thought it better that "a man should tyrannise over his bank balance than over his fellow-citizens."[18] This economistic conception of human life and society required two wondrous philosophical achievements. One is the modification of the traditional morality that condemned materialism and selfish pursuits. As the Skidelskys note, Bernard Mandeville and David Hume helped to redefine vice and virtue: "the old term 'avarice' was gradually sidelined in favor of the colorless 'self-interest.'"[19] Similarly, "Smith's doctrine of self-interest," they hold, "did more than just turn avarice into a virtue; it turned classical virtue into a vice. [. . .] Alms-giving was discouraged because it promoted idleness. Lust alone retained its deadly status."[20] It is perhaps not far-fetched to suggest that the theoretical neutralization of vices was probably a justification of the dominant cultural inclinations and preferences—that is, habits of the heart—and prevailing practices. Grotius' justification of the seizure of the Portuguese ship Santa Catarina in 1603 (whose cargo yielded more than three million Dutch guilders) illustrates this fascinating phenomenon.[21]

The following passage is an excerpt from Grotius' *De Jure Praedae Commentarius* (*Commentary on the Law of Prize and Booty*):

> Assuredly, too, the consuming greed for gain [. . .] is a vile disease of the spirit, characterized by complete disrespect for law and morality; yet it is possible to sin in contrary fashion, neglecting opportunities to promote one's own interests, through an anxious and overnice avoidance of things not essentially dishonourable. [. . .] In other words, let us not imagine that to be vicious which is devoid of vice; and let us not be unjust to ourselves while shunning injustice toward others. [. . .] Justice consists in taking a middle course. It is wrong to inflict injury, but it is also wrong to endure injury.[22]

The failure to seize the chance to enrich oneself now becomes a *sin*. It is significant that Grotius opportunistically quotes from authorities such as Homer, Lucretius, the Hebrew Bible, Plato, Aristotle, and Augustine to support his argument that being merciful or neglecting one's own interests is not necessarily just. It is therefore not surprising that he should cite Aristotle's definition of virtue as being the mean between two extremes (vices) but overlook the fact that Aristotle concluded that we cannot be unjust toward ourselves.[23] He also cleverly ignores the fact that Socrates (whom he cites) was convinced that it is better (more just) to suffer wrong than doing it if we must choose between the two.[24]

The second, related philosophical achievement is the seventeenth- and eighteenth-century idea that isolated individual actions driven by various interests—some of them being formerly "vices"—are spontaneously conducive to the public interest of society or should be made to become so through the right societal institutions. It is necessary to distinguish between two different versions of the general idea that individual interests do not lead to conflict but are instead wondrously turned into harmony by some "invisible hand." They reflect different conceptions of human motives. Taylor refers to Pierre Nicole's idea that society can be organized in such a manner that lower motives, too, serve it and to Mandeville's doggerel on the beehive that only thrives on vices.[25] Both Nicole and Mandeville were neo-Augustinians (or, to borrow a term of Taylor's, "hyper-Augustinians") who emphasized the depravity of human nature and did not believe that humans were able to transcend their "self-love."[26] Given this harsh reality, it is essential to ensure that self-love is put to uses that benefit society, for instance, by preventing boredom and idleness. Directly opposed to such religious pessimism is the Enlightenment belief that humans are capable of benevolence, or in any case, of decency. Such belief, however, as Taylor notes is born out of the experience of polite society among the elites. That experience is that "of success in imposing the order they [the elites] sought on themselves and on society. [. . .] the training in a disciplined, sober, industrious life came to be widespread enough that for lots of people this became a second nature."[27] In other words, the idea of the harmony of interests or an order of mutual benefits arises with the elites' increasing confidence in their project of civilization.

The civilizational project that primarily aims at making industrious and disciplined individuals is not the one Maritain had in mind. The democratic adventure is neither a military adventure nor an economistic adventure. It is not the ideal of bourgeois civilization praised by Carden and McCloskey, one that is "soaked with applied prudence."[28] Instead, as Maritain so eloquently writes, the "democratic philosophy of man and society has faith in the resources and the vocation of human nature. [. . .] It is therefore betting on heroism and the spiritual energies."[29] This, in full awareness of the power of evil. By aiming too high, we commit the old crime of hubris. But by aiming too low, we stifle the human spirit. It is perhaps not so surprising that both extremes have usually co-existed in Western societies. I referred earlier to Mumford's perceptive remark that the activation of the will-to-power might have been the result of a sense of inferiority. Despite the differences between the hyper-Augustinian and Enlightenment perspectives, they both lead to a stifling economism, in two important ways. First, by mocking and relativizing traditional morality, they destroy the ancient notion of limits and limited needs, thereby making us slaves to our disordered desires. And second, through the idea that the well-ordered *economic society* is self-stabilizing and thus not dependent on (illusory) virtues, they undermine all aspirations to a society based on civic friendship and justice. It is not very hard to see how the modern conception of self, morality, and society gives free rein to powerful economic forces to oppress the weak. As Polanyi writes, "harmony was inherent in the economy, it was said, the interests of the individual and the community being ultimately identical—but such harmonious self-regulation required that the individual should respect economic law even if it happened to destroy him."[30]

JUSTICE AS THE FULFILMENT OF NEEDS

Particular ideas, beliefs, and practices have got us where we are today. They can be criticized for being too parochial. Or, for simply being off the mark, either because they rely on an inadequate ontology that is disproved by our richest phenomenology, or because they have led to realities that do not match our richest ontology. We need actions directed to a common good or public interest that is comprehensive enough to include future generations worldwide.[31] These actions will involve sharing and sacrifice. Resistance is and will be great. "Ecomodernism" is an example of such resistance. As Clive Hamilton points out, ecomodernism continues "to pursue modernism's dream of using technology to bend nature to the will of humans."[32] Words to articulate the ways in which we, as individuals, families, communities, and nations, can surmount these all-too-human barriers are needed. We need a notion of justice that breaks with what Paula England calls a "separative model of human nature [. . .] because it presumes that humans are autonomous, impervious to social influences, and lack sufficient emotional connection to each other to make empathy possible."[33] A basic and simple idea of justice is espoused in the present work. It is a notion of justice that most of us implicitly embrace in our interaction with our dear ones. It is one that is thus motivated by love. The criteria for judging our thoughts, feelings, and actions (and nonactions) in these intimate contexts are rarely provided by formal laws (except in cases of obvious negligence or malice). We are unjust when we fail to assume our responsibilities toward our children, partners, parents, and friends, that is, when we fail to respond to their material and nonmaterial needs.

The willingness to assume the responsibility that is incumbent on us by virtue of our relationships is perhaps the most important manifestation of love. The desire for justice in these cases is the desire to meet the needs of our beloved ones, irrespective of their "merits," capacities, or virtues. Transposed to a higher level, the desire for justice becomes the desire to meet the needs of all our fellow beings, irrespective of their merits.[34] As Niebuhr so aptly writes, "there is no possibility of giving a rational definition of a just relation between man and man or nation and nation short of a complete love in which each life affirms the interests of the other."[35] As I will be arguing, that "complete love" that makes us feel responsible for strangers and for those whom we find repulsive—for instance, because of their views and ways of living—cannot be the affection that we feel for close friends. It can perhaps be best understood or imagined by recalling a situation when we no longer felt affection for someone but still felt responsible for her well-being, out of some kind of fidelity. Of course, in the case of strangers and those very different from us, there is no shared past and no shared memories. But the comparison may still be helpful because the commitment or fidelity to the well-being of the person to whom we no longer feel attached is no longer dependent on our personal feelings. This is one of the reasons why Buber speaks of the "metaphysical and metapsychical fact of love."[36] As he further explains, "love does not cling to the *I* in such a way as to have the *Thou* only for its 'content,' its object; but love is between *I* and *Thou*. [. . .] Love is responsibility of an *I* for a *Thou*." This phenomenology of love is metaphysical, religious, or poetic, but this does not make it sectarian, as I have noted earlier and will be arguing in the next pages. Our deepest experiences of love reveal its disruptive and transgressive character.

There are three (other) elements in my approach that might raise a few eyebrows and thus require further explaining. These are the introduction of the language of "needs," my emphasis on the "desire" for justice, and the lack of distinction between the private sphere and the politico-economic sphere (and correspondingly, between love and justice). Let me start with the third possible objection. It could be argued that my so-called simple definition of justice only applies to intimate contexts and cannot be transposed to the competitive arena of the political economy. My reply would be that I am in fact correcting a misconception by reuniting worlds that were never meant to be separated, at least not in democracies. Democracy, Maritain reminds us, is the ideal of fraternity. Similarly, Jean Bethke Elshtain writes that the dream of democracy "means sharing the possibility of a brotherhood and sisterhood that is perhaps fractious—as all brotherhoods and sisterhoods are—and yet united in a spirit that's a spirit more of good than ill will."[37] If we acknowledge this aspiration of the democratic project, then we, arguably, cannot bypass the notion of "needs" and escape the exacting justice of meeting the needs of all our brothers and sisters. That said, by re-introducing the language of needs and tying it up with justice, I may well be opening up a can of worms for several reasons. For one thing, "needs" is not a stable concept, and for another, there is an element of subjectivity attached to it. Ivan Illich therefore dismissed "needs" as "a social creation even more recent than work."[38] The needs of some are the luxuries of others.

Illich is certainly right in pointing out the creation of ever-increasing "needs." However, such a disastrous and enslaving spiral, I hold, is the result of having banned "needs" from our consciousness. There are three senses in which the language of needs can move us toward more justice. I have already referred to the first one. In a democracy, what is due to the other cannot be determined by "merits" or other qualities. As Mumford puts it,

> The claim to a livelihood rests upon the fact that, like the child in a family, one is a member of a community: the energy, the technical knowledge, the social heritage of a community belongs equally to every member of it, since in the large the individual contributions and differences are completely insignificant.[39]

In other words, in a political community, no one should be forced to struggle for existence on his or her own. Mumford's high standard of justice, which I am also defending here, rests on our conception of the bond that relates us to others. While we may disagree on the nature of that bond—and historically, we have certainly done so and are still doing so—our "metaphysical" disagreement may give way to more accord once we recognize the spirit of the democratic project. The latter is much older than Rousseau and Kant, as Maritain points out.[40]

The language of needs thus has both a positive and corrective function. It also has a normative function. There are absolute human needs of the human—material, intellectual, emotional, and spiritual—that cannot be ignored without great injustice. Once we start thinking in terms of needs, we must raise the tortuous question regarding these needs. As Buber remarked in 1952,

> The question one must proceed from will be this, apparently the simplest of all questions, yet inviting many difficulties: What does man need, every man, in order to live as a man? For if the globe is not to burst asunder, every man must be given what he needs for a really human life. Coming together out of hostile camps, those who stand in the authority of the spirit will dare to think with one another in terms of the whole planet.[41]

Buber speaks of "true needs" that must be recovered from "the exaggerations."[42] According to him, genuinely great political leaders get to know the true needs of their peoples and of other peoples. They are willing and able to think in terms of, and act for, the common good, that is, the good of a whole people and whole world. In the context of global and intergenerational justice, a consideration of the needs of other peoples forbids nations and corporations from usurping and destroying resources that other nations need to survive. Of course, I am describing a standard of justice that has been and is still being systematically transgressed. But this was precisely the reason why Buber retrieved that language of needs, urging us to rethink the essence of human existence and human fellowship.

The language of needs thus has the advantages of being affirmative, critical, and hence of setting limits that cannot be transgressed without injustice. Marcuse's distinction between "true and false needs" illustrates the critical and liberating potential of the concept:

> "False" are those [needs] which are superimposed upon the individual by particular social interests in his repression: the needs which perpetuate toil, aggressiveness, misery, and injustice. Their satisfaction might be most gratifying to the individual, but this happiness is not a condition which has to be maintained and protected if it serves to arrest the development of the ability (his own and others) to recognize the disease of the whole and grasp the chances of curing the disease. The result then is euphoria in unhappiness. Most of the prevailing needs to relax, to have fun, to behave and consume in accordance with the advertisements, to love and hate what others love and hate, belong to this category of false needs.[43]

This brings us back to the vicious spiral of economism and our willing enslavement to which Illich alludes. Marcuse makes it clear that the language of needs is not only relevant to matters of so-called distributive justice. This is also the reason why I do not think that "needs" competes with "capabilities" and "rights"; conversely, it means that the latter two concepts cannot simply replace the former. All three ideas are useful in particular contexts. "Needs," however, has a critical function that the other concepts do not have and, in this sense, is indispensable in our thinking about justice in the Anthropocene.

The language of needs, in the sense used by Marcuse, compels us to reexamine our culture and hence the structures of our political economies. This is also the meaning and scope of "needs" in Mumford's thought when he speaks of "the new economy of needs," in which whole economic processes will be humanized and industry will be "diverted from profit-making, private aggrandizement, crude exploitation."[44] People's struggles, worldwide, to survive, their (violent) struggles for recognition, ongoing wars, recurrent economic crises, and an imminent ecological disaster are telling signs that we have failed and are still failing to raise the question regarding our genuine needs. Peace, which was conceived to follow from prosperity, can only be dreamed of. Keynes was wrong to think that we would start to live in peace as we satisfied our "economic necessities."[45] Instead, as Schumacher remarked, we have to face the stark fact that "it is precisely the richest societies which pursue their economic advantage with the greatest ruthlessness."[46] Given this persisting history of narrow loyalties, it seems much more realistic to assume that self-concern, which includes the care for our immediate family and friends, is stronger than the care for others. Didn't Adam Smith recommend that we talk to others not of "our own necessities but of their advantages" if we wish to survive?[47] My argument is that this attitude is no realism at all but is a cultural phenomenon or ontological commitment that reflects our self-understanding. It is an attitude that belongs to the separative model of human nature.

I wish to distinguish between, on the one hand, our experience of our finite possibilities and, on the other hand, the belief that we cannot and should not strive beyond self-concern. Even if it were the case that we as individuals are generally only capable of narrow loyalties, there would be no rational reason to make such individual limitedness the absolute norm for a whole society, unless we have no faith at all in the possibility of moral growth. We clearly do have this faith since we still educate the young and try to change the behavior of adults through all kinds of therapies and training. Moreover, the civilizational drive to which I referred in previous pages clearly depends on that faith. So why are we reluctant to adopt the same standard of justice as the one that applies to intimate contexts when it comes to the politico-economic context? My argument is that such reluctance is culturally and hence ontologically informed. The reason why we find it difficult to accept the idea that we are responsible for strangers by virtue of our humanity is because we have been implicitly and unconsciously affirming an ontology in which we are competing individuals bound to each other by mutual interests and contracts. This image has very much realized itself. Our interactions are characterized by distance and impersonalism. As a result, it is much easier for powerful economic actors to trample weaker ones, for taxes to be evaded, and for toxic waste to be dumped in poorer countries and oceans without a qualm.

Our self-understanding is not easily changed since it is not a matter of simply changing our minds or even our theories of human nature. It is far too much of a habit of the heart and mind and informs far too many of our institutions. So even if we were to admit that our resistance to a more demanding standard of justice is culturally induced, it may still seem more workable to focus on the creation of just institutions and implement policies aimed at more equality than trying to enkindle love and the desire for justice in citizens. The language of fraternity or civic friendship is not the usual jargon of most politicians and policymakers. We have become accustomed to the idea that self-interest is not only unavoidable but also normal and legitimate. However, institutions and the successful implementation of policies aimed at more socioeconomic justice are dependent on our willingness to acknowledge the unconditional "worth" of the other. The best politico-economic institutions are bound to be ineffective if there is an insufficient acknowledgment of others as our fellow beings, that is, if a sense of fellowship is lacking. The ineffectiveness of institutions usually results in more monitoring mechanisms to contain the effects of a weak desire for justice. Genuine reforms that would put an end to a fundamentally undemocratic casino capitalism are still pending. Though this timidity can be blamed on the fact that no one gives up power and privileges voluntarily and on the subservience of politics to economic powers, we still ought to ask ourselves why there is a preference for power over justice.[48] What weakens our desire or will to be just, preventing us from choosing what we see to be the right thing to do, or from at all thinking and feeling in terms of right and wrong? This concern of mine underlies my focus on the "desire" for justice.

The weak desire for justice, I argue, can partly be blamed on our disordered passions, that is, a hierarchy of commitments or values that is in need of correction. Of course, the very idea that there are commitments that are essentially higher than others might be disputed. However, the varying degrees of the narrowness and homogeneity of our intimate circles and of our (un)willingness to expand these seem to confirm that premodern intuition. That said, the narrowness of our loyalties is not merely a personal failure. It is also fostered by particular cultural contexts and political climates. It is more tempting to take refuge in our own clans when we feel threatened by the "outside world," which has become too complicated and incomprehensible, or simply too different from what used to be familiar to us. This brings me to another reason for our lukewarm passion for justice, namely, the experience of the world as a cruel place where only the ruthless survive. Though such a world is far from being fictive, it did not arise despite ourselves. It is not a brute fact that has imposed itself on us. It is instead the product of our theories and practices, too. These have helped create an image of the world (or, of nature) as devoid of values and hence as either indifferent or cruel. Mumford astutely remarks that the "survival of the fittest" ideology was induced by the nineteenth-century social order and not so much by Darwin's work. The latter contains ideas of commensalism and symbiosis, which mitigate the "Victorian nightmare of a nature red in tooth and claw."[49] The historical and social context of Malthus and Darwin was one in which "only anti-social qualities had survival value. Only people who valued machines more than men were capable under these conditions of governing men to their own profit and advantage."[50] In such a world justice is a luxury that we cannot afford. We are too busy surviving to be concerned with others.

The conflict between utility and justice is a perennial one, masterfully articulated by Cicero in *De Re Publica* and *De Officiis*, for example. Justice would require the transcendence of our natural inclination to self-preservation, or less radically, a reconciliation of natural necessity and the demands of justice. Clearly, such a transcendence or reconciliation would require determining "natural necessity" and a critical re-evaluation of what we currently consider to be necessities. The question regarding needs is therefore double-edged. It not only obliges us to give to everyone what is necessary for a human life, but it also reintroduces the idea of limit. Along this line, the question of justice is not only about what we should get and give, but it is also about what we should give up. This brings me to a third reason for our weak passion for justice, namely, unlimited desires, that is, wants. The problem with wants (as opposed to needs) is that they have no limits since they are fueled by complex human passions and a boundless human imagination. The limitlessness of wants makes the clash between justice and wants even bigger than the one between justice and needs. Psychologically and philosophically speaking, the desire for justice is crowded out by much stronger desires, not only for material goods but also for prestige, status, and power. This phenomenon as such is not recent. What is peculiar to our times is that unlimited desires have been normalized and are even considered as being good for economic growth.

PHILOSOPHY, METAPHYSICS, AND RELIGION

A comparable emphasis on justice's dependence on love can be found in the works of Martha Nussbaum. Her *Political Emotions: Why Love Matters for Justice* (2013) is especially relevant to the present purpose. The focus on love follows quite naturally from a more integral or comprehensive humanism in which the whole human being (body, reason, and passions) and earthly, mortal life are fully affirmed. Similarly, in line with that same tradition, ideals are not conceived as self-sustaining. They demand our allegiance to be effective. We both try to identify that which fosters the human striving for justice and that which undermines it. Nussbaum rightly points out the alienating effects of competition and envy. "What we need as an antidote," she writes, "is a sense of a common fate, and a friendship that draws the advantaged and less advantaged into a single group, with a common task before it."[51] She goes to great lengths to find practical antidotes to our innate tendencies to deny our fellowship with other humans (and other beings). Her exploration and articulation of the resources that can help us affirm such fellowship within the constraints of the requirement of "neutrality" is an impressive example of philosophical tightrope walking. I share her worry about sectarianism and her commitment to neutrality but do not find her appeal to empirically oriented sciences to somehow replace the metaphysical underpinnings of her philosophical narrative very convincing. I do not think we can bypass theological and metaphysical ideas and intuitions, and I will show that Nussbaum herself provides us with a way out of this dilemma. There is a second aspect of her thought that is potentially restrictive, which is her "Aristotelian naturalism." The latter involves a conception of the human as another animal species (and less relevantly here, an opposition to notions of "transcendence"). But this limiting feature of her work is compensated by her recourse to Walt Whitman and Rabindranath Tagore

From a critical perspective, it could be argued that theological and metaphysical traditions have played too great a role in shaping a culture that is geared to domination to be ignored. They are also indirectly responsible for western positivism, as Max Horkheimer and Theodor W. Adorno have argued.[52] According to Horkheimer and Adorno, Enlightenment is the secularized form of Jewish monotheism. Both movements are driven by a demythologization urge.[53] The secular demythologization process has however backfired so that "even the concepts of mind, truth, and, indeed, enlightenment itself have been reduced to animistic magic."[54] Positivism has thus eradicated "thought" itself so that reason "has become merely an aid to the all-encompassing economic apparatus."[55] In a somewhat different manner and terminology, Taylor too, as I have shown, reconstructs a facet of the civilizational drive—partly religiously motivated—that results in disciplinary societies, "nomolatry," naturalistic materialism, and economism.[56] It therefore seems to me that if we wish to transcend a stifling and undemocratic economism and enkindle the love for justice, we must identify the religious and metaphysical assumptions or images that are in need of correction. Not surprisingly, these assumptions and images have informed apparently "secular" philosophies too since the latter necessarily bear the mark of the cultural context in which they emerged. For the present purpose, I would like to elaborate a little bit more on the two religiously inspired dimensions of the disembodied and disengaged self that have been so decisive for the separative model of human nature, namely, the Christian ambivalence toward bodiliness and religious individualism.

According to Mumford, we owe our "purposeless materialism" to the machine, which has made unlimited and mass consumption and production possible.[57] It is noteworthy that he writes that the machine and the servitude that it has entailed would most probably not have been possible without the "contempt for the body" enforced by "the institutions of the Church."[58] Moreover, it is significant that such contempt for the body was (is) most pronounced in milieus where the mastery of nature and self-mastery are commonplace (such as the monastery, mine, and the battlefield) and the least possible in agriculture (i.e., before its economization and technologization) due to its "life-conserving, life-maintaining functions."[59] Schumacher, similarly, writes that "the fundamental 'principle' of agriculture is that it deals with life, that is to say, with living substances."[60] Such contempt for, or fear of, the body, as I noted earlier, did not cease with the Protestant affirmation of ordinary, productive life. It is this aspect of a particular form of Christian culture that Nussbaum denounces, conceiving it as a "revulsion at the animality of the body."[61] Taylor speaks of "excarnation," which he considers as an "another monstrous creation of (corrupted) Christianity."[62] Christian individualism could be considered as an offshoot of such excarnation. Bodies and spirits can commune, but minds and disembodied souls typically do not. Christian individualism must be distinguished from the religious idea of individuality (i.e., of the unique "value" of every human being) and can thus best be understood as a form of religious atomism. Religious individualism is manifest in the Late Medieval emphasis on individual responsibility and individual sins and in Augustine's writings on predestination.

Given the long history of religious bigotry, triumphalism, exclusivism, and oppression, which are far from being a thing of the past, there are many reasons for being particularly critical of religious and metaphysical ideas, or for that matter, of any ideal that demands our full allegiance and love. But a *principled* repudiation of ideas and intuitions because they are associated with religious traditions is as unreasonable as the principled repudiation of ideas and intuitions by virtue of their having arisen in alien cultural contexts. I am not disputing the principle of "neutrality." In fact, I would be in favor of an even more radical form of neutrality, whereby the state is impartial to all conceptions of the good and understandings of human nature and, correspondingly, does not try to impose a particular self-understanding on all citizens. As Jocelyn Maclure and Charles Taylor note,

> This implies that the state should adopt a position of neutrality not only toward religions but also toward the different philosophical conceptions that stand as the secular equivalents of religions. In fact, a political system that replaces religion with a comprehensive secular philosophy as the foundation of its actions makes all the faithful members of a religion into second-class citizens, since these citizens do not embrace the reasons and evaluations enshrined in the officially recognized philosophy.[63]

Clearly, such neutrality is more theoretical than practical. In real life, policies and investments favor particular conceptions and ways of life. However, in a genuinely pluralist democracy, this aspiration to neutrality, which is also the aspiration to genuine dialogues, should be constantly recalled.

I certainly do think that ideas and beliefs can be sectarian, divisive, and oppressive. In our endeavors to explore and articulate the intuitions and attitudes that can help us to acknowledge others as our fellow beings and affirm their interests, our constant challenge is therefore to be aware of the cultural and personal biases inherent in all human endeavors, including philosophy and science. By appealing to empirically oriented sciences to legitimize her philosophical narrative, Nussbaum seems to be forgoing this radically critical philosophical attitude. She also seems to contradict her own project of affirming the reality of embodied reason when she implicitly (and most probably, unwittingly) attributes more "objectivity" to particular scientific methods. As Nussbaum writes:

> Cognitive psychologists during the past several decades have produced a wide range of excellent research on particular emotions, which, supplemented by the work of primatologists, anthropologists, neuroscientists, and psychoanalysts, gives us a lot of empirical data that are extremely useful to a normative philosophical project such as this one. Such empirical findings do not answer our normative questions, but they do help us to understand what may be impossible and what possible, what pervasive human tendencies may be harmful or helpful.[64]

It goes without saying that the question of human possibilities and impossibilities is itself a philosophical question that cannot be settled empirically since it pertains to the question of human nature. It is highly improbable that we shall be moved to acknowledge others as our fellow beings and accept responsibility for them once we know that they have the same needs and bodily excretions and exhibit similar behavior.

As I noted above, the capacity to accept responsibility for the stranger is perhaps the most important face of love. The idea that this capacity is defining for the human and, correspondingly, that to be human is to constantly ask "what is required of me?" is deeply religious *and* inclusive.[65] This question does not arise from the comparison with animals, and it is unlikely to arise in naturalistic philosophy. In fact, as Heschel points out, this Aristotelian method does not answer the fundamental question of who we are. As he writes,

> This tendency—so widespread in anthropological reflection—to comprehend man in comparison with the animal, for the perspective of what we know about the animal, is bound to yield answers which are unrelated to our question. [. . .] In asking the question about man our problem is not the undeniable fact of his animality but the enigma of what he does, because and in spite of, with and apart from, his animality.[66]

Moreover, it is dubious whether we really know the inner life of nonhuman animals. It is therefore surprising that Nussbaum claims that "no nonhuman animal denies that it is an animal, hates being an animal, shrinks from others of its kind because they are animals. None aspires to be an angel, above the body and its smells and fluids."[67] Is it also some kind of Aristotelian naturalism that informs Nussbaum's denial of the legitimacy of the human aspiration to be an angel? Partly. Another reason for her aversion to this image is that she thinks that it manifests the desire to be without a body. She thereby seems to overlook the possibility that the aspiration to transcend human nature may be part of human nature itself and that this transcendence does not necessarily consist in the denial of our bodiliness. By labeling this aspiration as an illusion, illegitimate, or pernicious, we no longer have the means to distinguish between wholesome and destructive ways of responding to this desire.

That said, religious, metaphysical, and mystical traditions do have a place in Nussbaum's thought. These ideas and images must, however, be properly translated and re-appropriated by poets and religious thinkers whose thoughts are marked by universalism.[68] Indeed, she quite rightly notes that there is no reason "not to turn to imaginative literature for illumination of human life, albeit with critical alertness, since literary works frequently prove sectarian, articulating some partisan religious or secular view of society's goals and purposes."[69] She therefore draws profusely on Whitman and Tagore, besides Sophocles, Aristotle, Rousseau, and Kant, among others. Obviously, there is a world of difference between the avowedly anti-metaphysical empiricists, on the one hand, and the writings of Whitman and Tagore, on the other.[70] So why draw the line when it comes to human nature and love? I propose we consider religious and metaphysical intuitions, ideas, and images on par with imaginative literature. When it comes to understanding ourselves, poetry and imaginative literature are of no lesser value and objectivity than science. In fact, they may be of greater value and objectivity since they are not a priori limited by prevailing cultural prejudices and scientific assumptions, norms, and methods. Of course, "critical alertness" does not only hold for imaginative literature. A critical engagement is also necessary with claims stemming from empirically oriented sciences, which are also theoretically, culturally, and hence metaphysically informed. As Schumacher remarks, "no system or machinery or economic doctrine or theory stands on its own feet: it is invariably built on a metaphysical foundation, that is to say upon man's basic outlook on life, its meaning and its purpose."[71]

Let us then assume that critical alertness is the fundamental attitude of the intellectual and scientist toward her own theoretical framework and cultural background (or background understanding), claims and ruminations about us humans, the nature of our relations with each other, with other beings, and with the world. The next question would then be about the nature of this critical engagement. How do we do it? Since these claims concern who we are and not, for instance, dark matter and atoms, we are well placed to evaluate them and judge whether they make sense to us from the first-person perspective. "Do I recognize myself in these definitions?"[72] The process of critical reflection is beautifully articulated by Taylor:

> What better measure of reality do we have in human affairs than those terms which on critical reflection and after correction of the errors we can detect make the best sense of our lives? "Making the best sense" here includes not only offering the best, most realistic orientation about the good but also allowing us best to understand and make sense of the actions and feelings of ourselves and others.[73]

We could add yet another evaluation criterion by asking to what extent particular accounts of humans and our worlds alienate us from ourselves, from our fellow beings, and from our world. Schumacher call these ideas a "bad, vicious, life-destroying type of metaphysics."[74] So adequately armed, there is no reason why we should eschew those terrifying religious and metaphysical traditions.

I am certainly not implying that a State should enforce particular "comprehensive doctrines" at the expense of others because these, for instance, happen to be our cultural legacy. That would contradict what Maritain referred to as the "pluralist principle."[75] A State, however, cannot be without foundation. In practice, there is thus a limit to the neutrality principle. As Nussbaum observes:

> The careful neutrality that a liberal state observes—and should observe—in matters of religion and comprehensive doctrine does not extend to the fundamentals of its own conception of justice (such as the equal worth of all citizens, the importance of certain fundamental rights, and the badness of various forms of discrimination and hierarchy).[76]

We need fundamental values to live a common political human life, and we could all probably agree on these fundamentals of the liberal state. (For the sake of argument, let us assume that patriarchists and racists are also on board because they are grateful for their freedom to have the wrong commitments). Do we then live happily ever after? Clearly not, as attested by Nussbaum's endeavor to reanimate the ideals of justice and civic friendship. Her liberal democratic project, however, is not only one of putting flesh on bare bones or fresh blood into a weakened democratic body. It also involves removing some old flesh and even some bones that have been preventing us from committing to civic friendship and justice.

The old flesh and bones are those rationalistic and individualistic prejudices that come with the liberal legacy. In other words, the fundamentals of the liberal state do not resolve the issue of constant interpretation and do not free us from the task of ensuring that certain readings of the fundamentals do not in fact contradict the pluralist principle. Economism and laissez-faireism are examples of such contradictions and are contrary to civic friendship and justice. But the problem is that they can be justified by the principle of freedom. We have here reached a stalemate because the liberal fundamentals do not tell us *why* we should commit to civic friendship, or *why* we should treat strangers as our equals, or *why* materialism is not proper to the human. These are metaphysical questions that we cannot avoid. Our commitments to pluralism, civic friendship, and justice confront us with the challenge of finding public languages to articulate both the resources for, and the obstacles to, justice and civic friendship. To this end, I do not see any reason to discriminate between religious and "nonreligious" ideas and intuitions. We could try to see them as our common pool of wisdoms that reflect the diversity of humankind, the richness of human experiences, and the fecundity of human thinking. The problem of the "translatability" of particular languages to a neutral or public language is not peculiar to religious writings (as any scholar will be able to confirm). Moreover, the extent to which we are able to understand alien ideas and intuitions also depends on our own capacity to understand otherness.

NOTES

1. John Maynard Keynes, *The General Theory of Employment, Interest, and Money* (Cham: Palgrave Macmillan, 2018), 140; Strange, *Casino Capitalism*; Robert Skidelsky and Edward Skidelsky, *How Much is Enough?: Money and the Good Life* (New York: Other Press, 2012), 181.
2. As Taylor explains: "To objectify a given domain is to deprive it of normative force for us, or at least to bracket the meanings it has for us in our lives. If we take a domain of being in which hitherto the way things are has defined meanings or set standards for us, and we now take a new stance towards it as neutral, without meaning or normative force, we can speak of objectifying it." Taylor, *A Secular Age*, 283.
3. See chapter two in Taylor, *A Secular Age*.
4. Mumford, *Technics and Civilization*, 43.
5. Polanyi, *The Great Transformation*, 57.
6. Mumford, *Technics and Civilization*, 20.
7. Bourdieu, *The Social Structures of the Economy*, 6.
8. Mumford, *Technics and Civilization*, 25.
9. Taylor, *A Secular Age*, 137.
10. Mumford, *Technics and Civilization*, 44.
11. Taylor, *A Secular Age*, 63.
12. Ibid, 266.
13. Polanyi, *The Great Transformation*, 35, 41.
14. Taylor, *A Secular Age*, 81–82.
15. Mumford, *Technics and Civilization*, 42–43.

16. Taylor, *A Secular Age*, 129.

17. Voltaire, *Lettres Philosophiques,* ed. Olivier Ferret and Antony McKenna (Paris: Classiques Garnier, 2010), 87.

18. Keynes, *The General Theory of Employment, Interest, and Money*, 333.

19. Skidelsky and Skidelsky, *How Much is Enough?*, 49.

20. Ibid, 50.

21. Martine Julia van Ittersum, "Hugo Grotius in Context: Van Heemskerck's Capture of the Santa Catarina and its Justification in De Jure Praedae (1604-1606)," *Asian Journal of Social Science* 31, no. 3 (2003): 531.

22. Hugo Grotius, *Commentary on the Law of Prize and Booty*, ed. Martine Julia van Ittersum (Indianapolis: Liberty Fund, 2006), 11–12.

23. Aristotle, *Nicomachean Ethics*, trans. H. Rackham (Cambridge, MA: Harvard University Press, 1926), 305–323 (Book V, ix–xi).

24. Plato, "Gorgias," in Plato, *Lysis-Symposium-Gorgias*, trans. W. R. M. Lamb (Cambridge, MA: Harvard University Press, 1925), 335–373 (469–479).

25. Taylor, *A Secular Age*, 229.

26. For a more thorough discussion of Nicole's and Mandeville's thinking with regard to self-love, see especially Chapter 6 ("Self-interest: the invisible hand of God") in Joost Hengstmengel, *Divine Providence in Early Modern Economic Thought* (London and New York: Routledge, 2019).

27. Taylor, *A Secular Age*, 228.

28. Carden and McCloskey, "The Bourgeois Deal," 43.

29. Maritain, *Christianity and Democracy*, 56.

30. Polanyi, *The Great Transformation*, 89.

31. The *res publica* ("commonwealth" or the "public thing") and the *bonum commune* (common good) are not completely synonymous but, for the present purpose, an explicit distinction is not necessary. For an elaborate analysis of the ambivalent concept "res publica," see Louise Hodgson, *Res Publica and the Roman Republic: "without Body or Form"* (Oxford: Oxford University Press, 2016). For Cicero, the *res publica* at times refers to that which constitutes a political community (a people), which includes a proper distribution of power. See Cicero, *On the Republic*, 47 (Book 1, 39).

32. Clive Hamilton, *Defiant Earth: The Fate of Humans in the Anthropocene* (Cambridge: Polity Press, 2017), 86.

33. Paula England, "The Separative Self: Androcentric Bias in Neoclassical Assumptions," in Marianne A. Ferber and Julie A. Nelson (eds.), *Beyond Economic Man: Feminist Theory and Economics* (Chicago: University of Chicago Press, 1993), 37.

34. For an evaluation of the merits and needs principles in our present context, see chapter six (on "Economic Responsibility"), from p. 123 onwards, in Opdebeeck, *The Economy and Meaningfulness*.

35. Reinhold Niebuhr, *Love and Justice: Selections from the Shorter Writings of Reinhold Niebuhr*, ed. D. B. Robertson (Louisville, KY: Westminster/John Knox Press, 1957), 50.

36. Martin Buber, *I and Thou*, trans. R. G. Smith (London: Bloomsbury, 2013 [1937]), 11.

37. Jean Bethke Elshtain, *Democracy on Trial* (New York: BasicBooks, 1995), 36.

38. Ivan Illich, *In the Mirror of the Past: Lectures and Addresses 1978-1990* (New York and London: Marion Boyars, 1992), 39.

39. Mumford. *Technics and Civilization*, 403.

40. Maritain, *Christianity and Democracy*, 49.

41. Martin Buber, *Pointing the Way: Collected Essays*, tran. and ed. M. Friedman (New York: Harper & Brothers, 1957), 228.

42. Ibid.

43. Marcuse, *One-Dimensional Man*, 7.

44. Mumford, *Technics and Civilization*, 412.

45. John Maynard Keynes, "Economic Possibilities for Our Grandchildren (1930)," in Elizabeth Johnson and Donald Moggridge (ed.), *The Collected Writings of John Maynard Keynes* (London: Royal Economic Society, 1978), 330–331.

46. Schumacher, *Small is Beautiful*, 33.

47. Adam Smith, *An Inquiry into the Nature and Causes of the Wealth of Nations*, Vol. 1 (Oxford: Clarendon Press, 1979), 27.

48. On the subservience of politics to financial powers, see, for instance, Coyle, *The Economics of Enough*, 244, 256; Simon Johnson, "The Quiet Coup," *The Atlantic* 1, May 2009, accessed April 30, 2021, https://www.theatlantic.com/magazine/archive/2009/05/the-quiet-coup/307364/.

49. Mumford, *Technics and Civilization*, 187.

50. Ibid.

51. Martha C. Nussbaum, *Political Emotions: Why Love Matters for Justice* (Cambridge, MA and London: The Belknap Press of Harvard University Press, 2013), 345.

52. Max Horkheimer and Theodor Adorno, *Dialectic of Enlightenment: Philosophical Fragments*, trans. Edmund Jephcott and ed. Gunzelin Schmid Noerr (Stanford, CA: Stanford University Press, 2002).

53. Such an "Enlightenment" endeavor is also discernible in Plato's *Euthyphro*, where Socrates asks his interlocutor whether he *really* believes that gods fight each other. See Plato, "Euthyphro," in *The Trial and Death of Socrates: Four Dialogues*, trans. Benjamin Jowett (New York: Dover Publications, 1992), 5. The demythologization urge is often conceived as an aspect of Axial and post-Axial religious and philosophical movements.

54. Horkheimer and Adorno, *Dialectic of Enlightenment*, 7, 11.

55. Ibid, 23.

56. Taylor, *A Secular Age*, 707.

57. Mumford, *Civilization and Technics*, 273.

58. Ibid, 35.

59. Mumford, *Technics and Civilization*, 35, 36.

60. Schumacher, *Small is Beautiful*, 101.

61. Nussbaum, *Political Emotions*, 140.

62. Taylor, *A Secular Age*, 741.

63. Jocelyn Maclure and Charles Taylor, *Secularism and Freedom of Conscience* (Cambridge, MA: Harvard University Press, 2011), 13–14.

64. Nussbaum, *Political Emotions*, 15–16.

65. Heschel, *Who is Man?*, 107.

66. Ibid, 21.

67. Nussbaum, *Political Emotions*, 159.

68. As she notes, "Thus [Martin Luther] King draws a lot of his imagery from the prophets (though also from Shakespeare and popular music); he uses those references, however, as a kind of civic poetry, and he makes it very clear that he looks to a future that includes everyone on a basis of equality. Gandhi, similarly, uses Hindu symbolism, but surrounds it with careful ritual gestures that emphasize the equality of Muslims and Christians." Nussbaum, *Political Emotions*, 387–388.

69. Nussbaum, *Political Emotions*, 138.

70. Not all empiricists claim to be anti-metaphysical. See Aaron Bruce Wilson, *Peirce's Empiricism: Its Roots and Its Originality* (Lanham, MD: Lexington Books, 2016), 282.

71. Schumacher, *Small is Beautiful*, 244.

72. Heschel, *Who is Man?*, 22.

73. Charles Taylor, *Sources of the Self: The Making of the Modern Identity* (Cambridge: Cambridge University Press, 1989), 57.

74. Schumacher, *Small is Beautiful*, 82.

75. Maritain, *Christianity and Democracy*, 180.

76. Nussbaum, *Political Emotions*, 7.

Chapter 2

The Primacy of Love

JUSTICE VERSUS LOVE?

Max Scheler thought it strange that the Christian idea of the priority of love over knowledge only very rarely found its way into philosophy and psychology.[1] Even less so into economic and political thinking, I would like to add. This was a remarkable fact for Scheler because he conceived that idea as belonging "to the essence of Christian consciousness and [to be] at the bottom of the church and all Christian ethics."[2] Christian philosophy, Scheler observes, has predominantly taken its cue from Greek philosophy. As a result, justice and freedom are conceived as being the products of the mind (reason). The primacy of reason (and knowledge) is implicitly and explicitly assumed. The uniqueness of Christian thought and experience, Scheler points out, lies in the reversal of the relationship between love and knowledge. Love is not the midwife that brings us to Perfect Being (Knowledge) and then disappears. It is instead intimately and ontologically related to that "Perfect Being" who is "perfect" not because of its impassibility but instead precisely because of its overabundant love. This reversal is splendidly captured by the title of Nussbaum's collection of essays, *Love's Knowledge*.[3] Yet, love seems to have been and to be predominantly the prerogative of poets, novelists, and mystics throughout the ages. It is thus not surprising that those thinkers who wish to enlarge and correct the ontology underpinning mainstream philosophy (and academia in general) have recourse to poetry and literature as sources of wisdom.

A more ambitious (and perhaps, more perilous) endeavor consists in integrating the idea of the primacy of love into the conceptual frameworks that guide our study of human realities and our thoughts on how to improve our practices. The proto-romantic movement initiated by Jean-Jacques Rousseau, the romantic movement itself, the phenomenological movement represented by Scheler, Jean-Luc Marion, Gabriel Marcel, Martin Buber, and Emmanuel Levinas exemplify such an endeavor. They are not immune to criticism, but they are commendable attempts to transcend the boundaries of a narrow rationalism. The objections to the proposition that justice can and ought to be rethought in terms of love, as it will appear, are valid mostly with respect to love conceived as a transient emotion and as charity. There is also the skeptical and cynical attitude that derides love as an illusion. Ironically enough, the only remedy for such skepticism and cynicism is love itself or, more precisely, the transformational experience of love. The greatest objection to my simple definition of justice is likely to pertain to the negation of the double standard of justice (and morality in general) that corresponds to the strict separation between the private sphere (family and friends) and outsiders (strangers). Such a move is not without its challenges, but, as it will appear, the latter are above all things of a practical rather than conceptual nature.

There are two objections that are of a conceptual nature, which I would like to address shortly here. These may appear to undermine the proposition that the best account of—as well as the highest form of—justice is one that is informed by the idea of the primacy of love, that is, by the notion that love is the telos of human existence. These objections, articulated by Hannah Arendt and, more recently, by Jean-Claude Kauffman are, firstly, that love is perverted and destroyed when it is mixed in worldly affairs; and secondly, that such mixture has disastrous consequences. Arendt asserts that love, "because of its inherent worldlessness [. . .] can only become false and perverted when it is used for political purposes such as the change or salvation of the world."[4] Similarly, Kaufmann asserts that "love quickly loses its soul when it decides to involve itself in the affairs of this world."[5] He moreover notes that "love's political projects [including the French Revolution] have always ended in failure."[6] "Love," he concludes, "was never meant to rule the world. Nothing can take the place of the clear, stable principles on which law and democracy are based."[7] Instead, love should confine itself to "promoting well-being by building thousands of houses of little pleasures."[8] For Arendt, the love between two lovers is "unworldly" and "antipolitical"—"perhaps the most powerful of all antipolitical human forces."[9] She goes on to argue that while love should not be taken out of its intimate context, respect, on the other hand, can be the basis for civic friendship since it does not involve intimacy.[10]

Arendt's emphasis on the unworldly nature of erotic love not only betrays the romantic conception of love but also strangely resembles the false mysticism that Scheler criticizes. Such mysticism consists in a love of the other that "leads one completely away from community" instead of bringing "one into increasingly deeper and more comprehensive communal relations with one's brethren."[11] True lovers are transformed by the love that relates them. Their love is expanded, the eyes of their hearts are enlightened, and they are thus enabled to include even more people in their immediate circles. We may therefore wonder whether the love, including the erotic and intimate love between lovers, that does not make us more responsive to the needs of those around us deserves to be called love at all. The first ecstatic moments that characterize the encounter between new lovers are normally succeeded by a more constant, mature (and often, self-giving) love. It is on this tranquil love, which involves—or perhaps, is—commitment that justice depends. Kaufmann captures this well in noting that "today's conjugal agape wants to be part of ordinary life. Passion, in contrast, still dreams of escaping it."[12] Yet, Kaufmann fails to see that the ideal of fraternity that presumedly motivated the great political experiments was either mixed with more abstract ideals (freedom and equality) or emptied of its substance because it was no longer embodied in real life. As Buber writes,

> The abstractions freedom and equality were held together there through the more concrete fraternity, for only if men feel themselves to be brothers can they partake of a genuine freedom from one another and a genuine equality with one another. But fraternity has been deprived of its original meaning, the relationship between children of God, and consequently of any real content. As a result, each of the two remaining watchwords was able to establish itself against the other and, by so doing, to wander farther and farther from its truth. Arrogant and presumptuous, each sucked into itself, ever more thoroughly, elements foreign to it, elements of passion for power and greed for possession.[13]

That love was no longer a "tranquil wisdom" as Kaufmann calls it.[14] His opposition between love and stable principles of justice is all the more surprising given his earlier distinction between that tranquil wisdom and the passion that makes us forget human reality. This is an important reason why such passionate "love" is viewed suspiciously in certain religious and philosophical traditions.

The conceived antithesis between love and justice recurs in various other works, including those of Christian thinkers. In the latter case, justice is defended against a version of love that involves submissiveness and passivity. Indeed, the Judaic-Christian love "commandment" may seem to introduce a tension between the love of God and neighbor, on the one hand, and the demand of justice, on the other. The oppressed are expected to bear their oppression, while (Christian) oppressors may think that they obey the commandment by giving alms from time to time or by engaging in philanthropy. As Niebuhr critically observes,

> The conscience of the Christian church has been confused by the tendency to substitute charity for justice through all the ages. [. . .] Whenever the love ideal

> of Christianity degenerates into pure philanthropy without regard for the difficult task of achieving social justice, it becomes a cloak behind which social injustice hides itself.[15]

The conflict here is not so much between love and (social) justice as between charity (in the popular sense of almsgiving) and justice. Philanthropy will always be necessary since poverty is most probably a fact of human existence. It is, however, not a substitute for the ideals of fraternity and justice. The problem of the concentration of wealth and power in the hands of the few cannot be solved by philanthropy. On the contrary, the latter can prevent genuine change by being a temporary sedative (Marx's famous opium).

AUGUSTINE'S MIXED LEGACY

According to certain readings of Augustine, the latter substituted the love of God and love of neighbor for justice.[16] It is noteworthy that subsequent thinkers, such as Gottfried Wilhelm Leibniz, Niebuhr, Paul Ricoeur, and Paul Tillich, addressed this issue.[17] As I have implied earlier, the opposition of justice to love makes sense only if we define love as an unstable emotion or as philanthropy. Yet, as Mary T. Clark rightly observes, Christian charity should not be confused with material donations to the needy.[18] Such almsgiving is called liberality, altruism, or philanthropy, which is not equivalent to Christian love, though it *might* be an expression of the latter. A more systematic interpretation of Augustine's thought reveals the dependence of justice on love. Justice is grounded upon love[19]; "love is the glue by which the divisions inside and outside each one of us can be corrected."[19] That said, Augustine provided reasons for the first interpretation and not only because he contradicted himself. Augustine, Scheler remarks, suffered from the influence of Neoplatonism, and from "his authoritarian will for unity of the church."[20] Love must be dissociated from all forms of monism. This is the metaphysical error that Scheler discerns in Plato, Indian thought, and mystics. Love in these traditions, according to Scheler's interpretation, is "no more than an intuitive knowledge of the unity of being [. . .] a movement toward each other of parts that were originally 'one and whole'."[21]

Augustine's anthropology and conception of order, in which oneness, unity, and a vertical hierarchy are preferred over and above partnership, equality, and dialogue, must be critically re-appraised. Only then can we make use of the positive elements of his legacy without adulterating either justice or love. Both Augustine's love of oneness and his patriarchalism are reflected in his exegesis of the story of Creation:

> God did not even wish to create the woman who was to be mated with man in the same way that He created man but, rather, out of him, in order that the whole human race might be derived entirely from one single individual.[22]

The same concern with one-ness and one right belief underlies Augustine's conviction that heretics should be deterred from the "evil of dissension" through punishments. To support his claim, he notes that "there is nothing better than to recall that single father of all our human race whom God created as a solitary individual, for the precise purpose of reminding us to preserve unity of heart in a multitude of men."[23] Augustine does not seem to have realized that this biblical interpretation is not so much an argument for as the result of the principle of oneness and unity. This is a strange lack of reflexivity for someone who is often applauded for being a profound psychologist avant la lettre.

Augustine's works can be used (and have been used) to maintain unjust conditions and to legitimize even the most tyrannical governments for the sake of unity and order. Since he believed that all power, even tyrannical power, came from God, he did not condemn the power structures of his time. Justice, for him, is in the first place the worship of God. Injustice is inherent to the human condition after the Fall. Though Augustine exhorted his audience to take care of the poor, he did not condemn the structures and institutions that caused poverty and inequalities; though he denounced the ill-treatment of slaves and did not deem it very Christian for Christians to possess slaves, he did not go so far as condemning that institution. Though he emphasized the dignity of the woman, the latter is in most of his works the helpmate of the man and only in that role the image of God. Augustine's controversial *uti* (to use)/*frui* (to "enjoy") principle, especially in relation to other living beings, has given rise to countless scholarship. His exposition of what it means to love God for his own sake and others for the sake of God in *De doctrina Christiana* shows the inadequacy of his terminology and logic. In sum, some of Augustine's thoughts are deeply problematic, both from a Christian perspective and from a nonreligious perspective. That said, it could still be argued that we owe the conceptualization of the primacy of love to Augustine and the Augustinian tradition.

Of course, the religious commandment of the love of God and neighbor is a notion that Augustine inherits. He is acquainted with various (non-Christian) traditions in which love plays a central role. His own merit is to have contributed to the foundation of a Christian anthropology and philosophy. According to Scheler,

> We find serious beginnings in conceptual understanding of the basic Christian experience of the relation of love to knowledge as well as to extrareligious

> problems solely in Augustine and the Augustinian tradition through Malebranche and Pascal. It is incorrect to attribute to Augustine a doctrine of the "primacy of the will" and to make him, in this respect, a precursor of Scotus. What is called primacy of will in Augustine is actually primacy of love. The act of love takes primacy not only over knowledge, but also over willing and striving. Love is simultaneously the primacy of taking an interest, as a lower stirring of "love," and the primacy of an act over other acts, such as perceiving, representing, remembering, and thinking—all of which mediate images and meaning contents.[24]

The insight regarding the precedence of love over knowledge helps us to understand why the "knowledge" of what is just can play no role in guiding our actions if we are not first moved by love to take interest in justice or, even more concretely, in those to whom justice is owed and to whom justice is denied.

It is indifference to the needs of others, the opposite of being interested, that sustains injustice. This indifference follows not so much from no love at all as from the wrong passions. Or, as Augustine says, lack of interest for the truly valuable is a sign of improperly ordered loves (commitments or loyalties). For him it is obvious that heavenly things are to be preferred to earthly things and that more lasting earthly things are to be preferred to transitory pleasures. According to him, if the wicked could have both wisdom and money, he would take both. It is only when he must choose one of them that he prefers that which is less valuable.[25] The wicked is therefore the person who has got his priorities wrong. He attributes more value to what is intrinsically less valuable and less value to what is intrinsically more valuable. Perhaps even more importantly, he makes the wrong choices because he is too weak to resist temptation. Augustine observes that if we were asked to choose between justice and money—theoretically—we would choose justice because justice is more beautiful and praiseworthy. We know that justice is to be preferred to money. However, in the real world, that knowledge does not help when temptation comes along. Augustine writes:

> It [temptation] offers you some money from somewhere else. Now temptation is saying to you: "Look, here's some money you could have; if you do a bit of cheating the money is yours." But justice will ask you, "What are you going to choose? Now's my chance to test your words." When you were listening to my questions just before, you preferred justice to money. But now—both of them are in front of you! Money on this side; justice on that side. You close your eyes against justice, as if you are ashamed, and you stretch out your hand to take the money.[26]

We can conclude that it is weakness that often makes us unjust. In later chapters, I address the question of how we can become "strong" enough to choose justice even if it happens to harm our immediate interests.

The implication of the law of love for justice becomes evident in contexts where unjust conditions are allowed to perpetuate themselves lawfully. In the socioeconomic context, unjust prices, determined by the market, are legal. The modern ambition of making comfort and luxuries available to all has taken its toll. For example, slave wages at the beginning of supply chains are common in many sectors. These workers are paid their "due" determined by the market. The market, however, gets it wrong for many reasons. I will come back to this issue in later chapters. This means that though there is no violation of formal laws, there is injustice. The law of love, on the other hand, demands from us that we transcend the prevailing norms of what appears to be just. In the case of slave wages, we are urged to consider the needs of workers, who are above all things our fellow beings. So it is not simply the case that we are being asked to consider those who are exploited as "ends" instead of "means." The law of love calls on us to consider ourselves related to these strangers by an invisible bond of love and to give to them what is due to them in accordance with the demands of this relation. The implications of a higher standard justice are well illustrated by Augustine's engagement with Cicero. The latter seems to have believed that there was once justice among the Romans and that justice was lost through the "depraved opinions of men," bad leadership, wandering citizens who preferred trade to the cultivation of land and military service, and the taste for comfort and luxury.[27] Though Augustine agrees with Cicero on several accounts and endorses many of his insights, we see a tension between Augustine's universalism and Cicero's patriotism.

Augustine's claim that Rome was never a republic because true justice (found where the true God is worshipped) was never practiced is well known.[28] I would now like to look at the divergent ways in which the kidnapping of the Sabine women is narrated by these two men. They reveal the clash between narrow loyalties (the flourishing of one's own homeland) and a broader loyalty. While the historical episode of the abduction of the Sabine women under the reign of Romulus is narrated quite matter-of-factly in Cicero's *De Re Publica*, Augustine's lengthy exposition of this early period of Rome unequivocally reflects his moral indignation and hence his commitment to the higher law of love. According to Cicero,

> [Romulus] ordered the seizure of the Sabine maidens, born of honorable lineage, who had come to Rome for the games (which he had then begun for the first time to make annual, during the Consualia in the circus), and he had them married into the most distinguished families.[29]

Augustine, on the other hand, in reply to Sallust's (and Cicero's) claim that natural justice and morality flourished among the Romans, observes ironically:

> I presume, then, that it was this natural justice and morality that explains the rape of the Sabine women![30] What could be more just and moral than that other people's daughters should be decoyed under pretense of a circus and then, not by parental consent, but by violence, be snatched away by anyone who could! If the Sabines did wrong in refusing to surrender their daughters upon demand how much greater was the wrong in seizing them when not surrendered? It was more just, one must suppose, to go to war with a people for refusing to give their daughters in marriage to their countrymen and neighbors who had requested them, than with a people who demanded that their stolen daughters be restored![31]

We might say that it was easy for Augustine to condemn this early Roman practice since such criticism served to reinforce the idea that justice is only possible in the City of God.[32] The above discussion nevertheless illustrates the clash between loyalties and the much broader loyalty implied by the law of love. The latter reminds us of basic principles of justice in times of chaos when survival or growth gets all our attention.

It is not always easy to see a champion of justice in Augustine. He perceived feeding the hungry and sheltering the homeless as works of *mercy* and not as justice.[33] Such inadequacy can be blamed on his inherited conceptual framework, which he at times did manage to surpass. Trained in the science of argumentation (to which philosophy is sometimes reduced), the younger Augustine was keen to win debates. In his early works (such as *De Ordine*), he applied these philosophical methods to the question of God. Against the sceptics (the Academics) of his time, he deemed the happy life possible. The older Augustine becomes more critical of his previous endeavors and beliefs. He observes that this earthly life cannot be called happy.[34] Wars and injustices show the wretchedness of the human condition. Unless we have hearts of stone, there is no way we can be "happy" simply by taking pleasure in our own virtues while being surrounded by calamities. Though such a change of mind can be explained by changing circumstances, by richer experiences and griefs, it is also the result of Augustine's internalization of the primacy of love. Yet, he did not work out the full implications of the primacy of love for justice. Had he done so, he would have emphasized our responsibility for others, which follows from the communion of fellow beings. Niebuhr, who has critically re-appraised and re-appropriated the Augustinian legacy, is able to avoid both the degeneration of love into charity and what he calls religious sentimentalism. Let us now turn to his conceptualization of the highest law of human life.

BETWEEN IDEALISM AND FATALISM

In his earlier works, Niebuhr argues that the endeavor to transfer the ideal of individual moral perfection to intergroup relations is bound to fail. Modern religious and secular idealism, he observes, is oblivious to the clash between individual morality and collective immorality. Hence, while individual egoism can be transformed to some extent, collective egoism is closed to such moral discipline.[35] As Niebuhr observes, "the selfishness of nations is proverbial."[36] Despite this emphasis on human egoism, he does not share the Lutheran and Hobbesian pessimism. In fact, Hobbes did not understand the true tragedy of human existence (and Luther underestimated the immanence of divine love). Human creatures are tragic creatures because they are caught between finitude and the infinite. Their yearning for the universal and absolute expresses itself in the constant search for universal values but also in ascribing universal validity to their partial views. The latter tendency corresponds to the imperialist will to dominate, which is a perverse consequence of the human capacity for freedom and self-transcendence. This will-to-power is the manifestation of human "sin," which, according to Niebuhr, is perhaps the only empirically verifiable claim of Christianity. Sin is the perversion of the "natural will-to-live into an imperial will-to-power";[37] it is the "false eternal and the false universal."[38] It is thus not an inherited condition but rather the proof of human freedom. This conception of "original sin" as non-historical, that is, as having no history (no beginning) is one of the many purifications of religion undertaken by Niebuhr. The lucid awareness of ineradicable evil, however, is no reason for fatalism. On the contrary, Niebuhr has tirelessly criticized the complacency that stems from both pessimism and optimism.

Judging from several of his works, it may appear that, for Niebuhr, any attempt to re-organize our economic life by having recourse to the law or ethic of love can be considered as self-deception at best and unjust at worst. Self-deception it would be since one would underestimate the power of egoism and lust for power in what may seem to be expressions of love. "Ruthless power," Niebuhr points out, "operates behind a screen of pretended ideal ends."[39] Similarly, injustice is sustained and reinforced when an unjust social order is not criticized but made even more bearable by philanthropy, which, moreover, is rarely exempt from selfishness, pride, and the feeling of superiority. We need mechanisms of social justice because we cannot rely on the present and future "goodwill" of "educated" people for basic justice. Competing interests and unhealthy concentrations of powers cannot be resolved by preaching the love of one another: "no moral idealism can overcome a basic mechanical defect in the social structure."[40] In earlier works, Niebuhr therefore stresses the necessity of coercion by law, checks and balances, and the socialization of economic power in order to minimize injustices. At the same time, he warns that coercion can serve "the purposes of the coercing power rather than the general weal."[41] Niebuhr ends his *Moral Man and Immoral Society* on a tragic note:

> We live in an age in which personal moral idealism is easily accused of hypocrisy and frequently deserves it. It is an age in which honesty is possible only when it skirts the edges of cynicism. All this is rather tragic. For what the individual conscience feels when it lifts itself above the world of nature and the system of collective relationships in which the human spirit remains under the power of nature, is not a luxury but a necessity of the soul. [Yet] we cannot build our individual ladders to heaven and leave the total human enterprise unredeemed of its excesses and corruptions.[42]

The awareness of the tragic tension between the individual striving for justice, on the one hand, and the collective will-to-power, on the other, never disappears from Niebuhr's works. In his later writings, however, we see the growing awareness that love in the world takes different forms and that a sense of justice is one of the faces of love. Niebuhr also realizes that the socialization of economic power may not be the solution to the concentration of power. He notes that "the Marxist theory wrongly assumes that economic power inheres solely in the ownership of property and obscures the power of the manager of property."[43] Instead, in socialized concerns, the power is shifted to managerial oligarchs. The problem of concentration of power repeats itself in a different way. Power must therefore "be held under democratic restraints because irresponsible power is always dangerous. It is dangerous because a dominant oligarchy always pretends a false identity between its interests and the general welfare."[44] Democratic institutions, however, are not sufficient for such restraints. Economism precisely means that whole democracies are held hostage by private, economic, and financial powers. Corporate blackmail is an explicit form of such bondage. A more insidious undermining of democracies consists in the subordination of political thinking to economic concerns. The more comprehensive ends that the economy is meant to serve are thereby erased from public consciousness. Successful democratic processes are dependent on equality, rationality (reasonableness), and the capacity to think in terms of the common good of the people today and tomorrow and ideally, of other peoples as well.

Clear and stable principles become a dead letter when people are unwilling or incapable of obeying what Niebuhr calls the "ultimate law of life," which is the "law of love," that is, when we do not respond to the call of loving others as we love ourselves.[45] This law of love is as universal as Kant's moral law and is therefore not merely subjective or personal. Love understood this way is more than a human experience. It is also the "mystery" behind and above the tragic world.[46] It is its very meaning. This means that the law of love also judges the various manifestations of our love. Indeed, the law of love transcends not only ordinary selfishness but also very "natural" forms of love, such as family love and patriotism. The love of one's own kin can prevent higher and more inclusive commitments by monopolizing our attention, time, and energy. But also, egoism rarely manifests itself in purely individual pursuits.[47] The devotion to our family, corporation, party, or nation can become a form of "sublimated egoism," being the projection of our own ego.[48] The profoundest existential wisdom involves an awareness of the tension between the highest human aspirations to inclusion, on the one hand, and the many faces of human egoism, on the other. It reveals the subtle human evils that insinuate themselves into the most intimate human relationships that are seemingly constituted by love or friendship. Love conceived as the power that makes the world go round is one that also "purifies" and stabilizes our natural emotions of sympathy, compassion, and friendship. I will elaborate on this interaction between love as an emotion and love as an extra-human power in the next chapter.

Hence, the ideal of love cannot be dismissed as too religiously particular to be of relevance to the non-initiated. As Niebuhr points out, the idea of love as the ultimate moral vocation of all humans is not merely a "caprice of mythology."[49] It is not held true because it is "revealed." On the contrary, the cross "symbolizes an ideal which establishes points of relevance with the deepest experiences and insights of human life."[50] The ethic of love thus competes with the rationalist (Stoic and Kantian) approach to human morality, in which the emphasis is laid on reason and duty. In both the religious-moralist and the rationalist approaches, universalism is striven after, against natural—and often narrow—loyalties. Niebuhr thus explains:

> A rational ethic seeks to bring the needs of others into equal consideration with those of the self. The religious ethic [. . .] insists that the needs of the neighbor shall be met, without a careful computation of relative needs. This emphasis upon love is another fruit of the religious sense of the absolute. [. . .] Love meets the needs of the neighbor, without carefully weighing and comparing his needs with those of the self. It is therefore ethically purer than the justice which is prompted by reason.[51]

Love as an ideal may be ethically purer, but this clearly does not make it possible in practice. The ethic of love is extremely demanding, and as Niebuhr tirelessly points out, too many corrupted versions of that ethic have maintained unjust status quos. It is very much an impossible possibility, and in certain situations, requires from us that we sacrifice our own interests for the sake of strangers.

While it is obvious that philanthropy or charity (alms) does not necessarily reflect, and is not equivalent to, agapeic love, sacrifices do tend to suggest its influence. We may be inclined to see the manifestation of agapeic love in the entrepreneur who sacrifices short-term profits for the sake of better working conditions for his (her) employees, for instance. Such decisions and actions should certainly not be denigrated since they contribute to the greater well-being of those involved. However, such sacrifice is not necessarily agapeic in the strict sense of the term. It is more correct to see it as a "prudential sacrifice," which Niebuhr refers to as the "bourgeois version of sacrifice," a "sacrifice that is advantageous in the long-run."[52] In other words, there is calculation, a cost-benefit analysis involved. Though such version of sacrifice is to be preferred to the fixation on short-term profits at any cost, it should not be allowed to overshadow the radicalism, absolutism, and hence unprudential character of agapeic love. "Highest mutuality," says Niebuhr, "is achieved where mutual advantages are not consciously sought as the fruit of love. For love is purest where it desires no returns for itself; and it is most potent where it is purest."[53] The tension between the religious ethic and our competitive socioeconomic life cannot be fully resolved.

For the religious person, the permanent temptation of narrow loyalties and the will-to-power is no reason for despair because humans are not alone.[54] The "good news," Niebuhr points out, is that divine mercy can help us "overcome a contradiction within our own souls, which we cannot ourselves overcome."[55] This means that an ethic of pure disinterestedness is impossible if we think that we are condemned to rely exclusively on human forces. This "realism" underlies the philosophy of Hobbes and of those religious thinkers who have emphasized God's transcendence at the expense of his immanence, and of all those who have ousted God from the world. Secular utopias are dangerous precisely because they do not endorse this realism and demand more from human selves than they can possibly offer. Religious utopias, of course, run the same risk if they exclude divine love in theory and practice. Are the nonreligious among us then compelled to be "realists" and to accept that we cannot and should not aim too high? Christian theologians have tended to narrow the realm of divine love (grace). While God is thought to make the sun shine upon all equally, he is purportedly more selective when it comes to his transformational love. Niebuhr does not seem to choose that narrow path, and he could not possibly do so since he is constantly addressing himself to a secular audience (and the socially oppressed who feel betrayed by the church).

If the extra-human power attested to by religious traditions, poetry, and literature—and our "best phenomenology" to borrow Taylor's terminology once again—is involved in all human lives in very intimate and mysterious ways, then there is no reason why it should confine itself to a select few and bypass the nonreligious receptive to it. Being "nonreligious," however, must be further qualified. While it does not involve a commitment to organized religions and theological theories, it does entail "piety." I will come back to that "piety" or "primary religion" in chapter 5. It is the attitude of humble and thinking persons who have "reverence for the mystery and the majesty that transcend all human knowledge."[56] This attitude, which, in a robust sense, is the precondition for the love of wisdom (philosophy), is also the best antidote to the temptation to objectify any extra-human power that may be available to us, and it should guard us against the illusion that we are able to manipulate such power. If this language still sounds (unpleasantly) religious, "premodern," and "unnatural," then we should blame our culture for having stifled our esprit de finesse, for having made us insensitive to subtle languages, and simply for having made us insensitive to our surroundings (that is, for having turned us into "buffered selves").

THE MOTIVE POWER OF THE INFINITE

The theological complications that I touched upon above are absent in the works of Buber, to whose understanding of love I will now turn. The vertical hierarchy of Augustine gives way to relationality and partnership. Augustine's unfortunate claim that only God is to be enjoyed and the rest "used" is greatly relativized when we learn to see the world through the eyes of love.[57] During those rare moments, the sense of connectedness with the "things" devoid of reason and beings with lesser rationality overrules the notion that we have dominion over the world. The humanness of the human being lies in his (her) capacity "to come into direct contact with everything that he bodily or spiritually meets—to address it with lips and heart or even with the heart alone."[58] It is thus our capacity to approach the other as a fellow being or comrade that qualifies us as being human. The love of the world (reminiscent of Arendt's *amor mundi*) is the love of an unredeemed world where humans sway between the "will to enter into relation" and the will to profit and power.[59] It is noteworthy that Buber stresses the necessity of not so much destroying the will to profit and power as balancing it by the spirit that says Thou. In other words, economics (as well as politics) must be grounded in mutuality. This emphasis on mutuality and dialogue does not replace the commandment of love, but it constitutes a qualification of love. Genuine love manifests itself in dialogue, rightly understood. Dialogue, as I show here, has a spiritual dimension and demands a lot from us. It should not be confused with the Socratic dialogues since there is no argument to be won.

I referred earlier to Buber's conception of love as metaphysical and metapsychical. He is therefore reluctant to conceive love as a feeling. He thus notes that he knows no one "who has succeeded in loving every man he met."[60] Dialogue, on the other hand, should be at the heart of human life. It consists in directing one's attention to the other with one's whole being. Buber is known for his philosophy of dialogue and not so much for some version of the law of love. He considered his *I and Thou* as representative of his thought. In this little book of his, the reader is introduced to the life of dialogue. In living the life of dialogue, we distance ourselves from approaching the other as an "It," a being or thing that we can use. Yet, dialogue is not simply about treating the other as an end. In a strong sense, Buber transcends the means-ends paradigm, just as he transcends Augustine's *uti/frui* duality. We become who we should be through the many little encounters with other beings and things during the course of our lives.[61] We are all called to maintain a "holy intercourse with the little world entrusted" to each one of us.[62] This is how we "help the holy spiritual substance" contained in living beings and things, including the tools we use, "to accomplish itself in that section of Creation in which we are living."[63] For the religious person this entails accepting the responsibility of being God's partner in creation: action becomes "purposive" and yet "is no longer imposed upon the world, it grows on it as if it were non-action."[64] For both the religious and the nonreligious person addressing the other as Thou means accepting the responsibility for him or her. Fellowship, mutuality, and responsibility for each other are therefore the core concepts that are attached to the I-Thou relation.

The dialogical approach may seem less confusing and elusive than the language of love and more applicable to our socioeconomic and political contexts. That impression of unambiguity should be quickly dispelled when we read what Buber has to say about mutuality:

> In the deadly crush of an air-raid shelter the glances of two strangers suddenly meet for a second in astonishing and unrelated mutuality; when the All Clear sounds it is forgotten; and yet it did happen. [. . .] In the understanding of such fleeting and yet consistent happenings one must guard against introducing motives of feeling: what happens here cannot be reached by psychological concepts, it is something ontic.[65]

Let us compare that fragment with what he writes about love:

> Feelings accompany the metaphysical and metapsychical fact of love, but they do not constitute it. The accompanying feelings can be of greatly differing kinds. [. . .] Feelings dwell in man; but man dwells in his love. That is no metaphor, but the actual truth.[66]

Both the dialogical event and love do not let themselves be captured and fully defined. It is significant that the first pages of *I and Thou*—meant to be an introduction to the life of dialogue—is about the love between I and Thou. It is the same cosmic love that runs through the world.

There is reason to hold that Buber's recourse to dialogue is not an alternative to love but instead a concretization of the highest law of human life. It is also a correction of the misconceptions of love and corresponding practices. Buber thus notes that "love without dialogic, without real outgoing to the other, reaching to the other, and companying with the other, the love remaining with itself—this is called Lucifer."[67] That is the love of the individual who loves humanity without loving concrete persons or loves God without real encounters with people in the real world. As we saw above, Buber goes to great pains to dissociate both love and dialogue from feelings. We cannot be commanded to feel affection for the "evil man," but we are responsible for him (her).[68] Love is the "cosmic and eternal power" that can be found in the "callousness of one's fellow humans beings";[69] it can "redeem the crowd into men and strike even the heart of the crude, the greedy, [and] the stingy."[70] Love, in this sense, is what Catherine Osborne calls an "external cause of loving relationships."[71] It must be considered as a motive and not as "a response provoked by some object."[72] Love as a motive thus exists among other motives. The person who chooses love as a motive, that is, as her existential attitude, gives up the motives of gain and power for what Buber calls the "motive power of the infinite" and, accordingly, accepts the responsibility for the "whole untraceable world-event."[73]

Love is a power that causes affection while it itself is not that affection. It makes relationships last but is not identical with that relationship.[74] The latter relationship dwells in that love, just as the person dwells in love. That power, usually associated with a god or God, is both transcendent and immanent. This explains Buber's poetic and rather apophatic language. Since love envelops us, we cannot objectify it. We can discern some of its workings but not all of them. Any definition threatens to reduce it to our own measure. It is nonetheless possible to say something about the place of love in our world. It is possible to make a claim regarding the primacy of love. Similarly to Scheler (and his reconceptualization of the Augustinian tradition), Buber holds that love precedes and enables the true knowledge of the world, true art, true science, true philosophy, and every true deed. That knowledge is the one that follows from embracing the beloved (either world or another being) and is thus not the result of dissection and categorization. The knower is not the spectator or observer but exposes his (her) self—whole being—to that which s(he) tries to understand. This approach stands in stark contrast to the ambition of impersonalism that underlies modern science. The "effective reality" of things reveals itself only to those who lovingly approach them.[75]

Authentic art, science, and philosophy depend on the love of artist, scientist, and philosopher, respectively, that is, on their willingness to see things through the eyes of love. The latter expression may not be adequate to capture the involvement of their whole being in this process of discovery. The loving and hence authentic artist experiences the beloved thing with his whole self and therefore "feels its outlines with his limbs."[76] He discovers the beauty of things, pays tribute and gives shape to it through his work. The latter is an invitation to others to experience the hidden beauty of those same things. The loving scientist is initiated into the secret life of things. She experiences them as happenings rather than passive objects to be studied. She shares her science with others using concepts that do justice to the reality that she has had the privilege of encountering. In a strong sense, the privilege and hence responsibility of the loving philosopher is even greater since things reveal their meanings and laws to her.[77] The experience of, or encounter with, that meaning is disruptive and shatters her taken-for-granted assumptions.

The precondition of love for authenticity and thus truth does not only hold for the artist, scientist, and philosopher. Every small or great action is true if it is performed by a loving person. As Buber writes:

> Every true deed is a loving deed. All true deeds arise from contact with a beloved thing and flow into the universe. Any true deed brings, out of lived unity, unity into the world. Unity is not a property of the world but its task. To form unity out of the world is our never-ending work.[78]

The loving person who acts in the world with his whole and united self contributes to the redemption of that world. The deeds of such unified selves are true and healing deeds that foster genuine peace, which is not simply a temporary state of nonwar and of balance of powers. Unified selves can engage in a genuine dialogue and are attentive to each other's needs. The loving person asks himself the question, "What have I to do" with all his soul and hears the "old eternal answer": "You shall not withhold yourself."[79] Only when unified selves meet other unified selves is there hope for peace and justice. The notion of unified selves is an important aspect of both Buber's and Niebuhr's thoughts, to which I will come back in the next chapter. For the time being, it suffices to note that every person, whether a CEO or a caretaker, who lovingly addresses everything and everyone with lips or only with the heart gets a glimpse of eternity. Reverence and humility characterize the disposition of such a person.

TENSIONS AND CONFLICTS

In the writings of both Niebuhr and Buber, we see that love is the cosmic and eternal power that is readily available to those who are willing to remain in it, and they do so when they choose the motive of love above other motives. There is what Niebuhr calls a "curious compound of willing through the strength of the sense of obligation and of willing not by the strength of our will but by the strength which enters the will through grace."[80] There are two questions that I would like to address here. One is whether we need the notion of grace or divine love at all. Buber's philosophy of dialogue may appear more attractive and to have more universal import precisely because he avoids theological controversies. However, it is one thing to avoid theological controversies and quite another to deny the involvement of divine love in human affairs. For Buber, the unity of the self, as we shall see later, is not possible without "the divine force" in the depths of the soul.[81] The divine force is in the depths of all souls. As I suggested above, there is no reason to assume that Niebuhr would object to the idea that divine love is available to all. This brings me to the second matter, which regards the gap between personal morality (justice) and justice at the collective level. Even if we were to accept the idea that the just self is the unified self and that such unity can be reached through the divine force within it, it is still not clear how just selves lead to justice at the collective level. This would have been the case in an imaginary world in which all selves directly interact with each other, without impersonal mediation. But contemporary technological societies are impersonal and bureaucratized. The organizational preference for vastness, impersonalism, and anonymity, the habit of thinking in terms of abstractions and statistics have contributed to undermining the immediacy between persons and our capacity (or goodwill) to see our fellow beings as our equals.

A conversation between Niebuhr and Buber on this matter is quite illuminating. The two men knew and corresponded with each other. Though Niebuhr held Buber in great esteem, he was (at times) critical of the idea that the dialogical approach—which is between persons—could be transposed to the economic and political levels. Niebuhr thus writes:

> I think it is slightly ironic that he [Buber] should have such a rigorous personal, not to say individualistic, interpretation of human relations, when I have always regarded Hebrew thought superior to Christian thought because it had the norm of justice rather than the norm of love, or rather it had two norms of justice and love, while Christian thought always tended to be perfectionist in terms of the love doctrine.[82]

In reaction to this criticism, Buber replies:

> I am a meliorist and not an idealist, and so I want only as much dialogic element as can be realized in human life here and now. The real strength of "collective

> relations" depends on the strength of the personal relations involved in them. [. . .] There is no "norm of love" at all. The commandment of love cannot command other than to be ready to love and willing to act lovingly "with all thy soul." But there is indeed a norm of justice.[83]

Buber goes on to add that society, in order to be a humane living environment, must be based on interpersonal relations. More precisely, societies much be organized in such ways as to allow direct, interpersonal relations. For Buber, the "artfully constructed equilibria of power" might guarantee order but not justice. Justice cannot mean anything else other than "being just."[84] Elsewhere, he points out that Niebuhr is "interested in society as an institutional reality and I [Buber] as a relational one."[85] Different conceptions of society arguably divide those who conceive (socioeconomic) justice and love as intimately connected and those who conceive justice as a balance of powers. This is however only partly the reason for the disagreement between Buber and Niebuhr, a disagreement that becomes less pronounced in Niebuhr's later works. As I remarked earlier, the latter tends to emphasize the importance of justice as opposed to love in his early writings in reaction to misconceptions of the law of love (and even more importantly, practices legitimized by these misconceptions). Both Niebuhr and Buber believe that humans are called to fellowship with each other and that societies *ought to be* organized in such ways as to foster such fellowship. They share the same vision of what human societies ought to be and realize that societies are far away from that ideal. Both deplore the lack of organic unity between fellow beings. In the next chapters, I will be looking at some of the factors that impede dialogical life.

That said, the conceived tension between personal morality (and hence personal aspirations to justice) and collective life seems to be more pronounced in Niebuhr's work. Collective life is the realm of the will-to-power and to profit. In such a context, we might harm ourselves by trying to be just. We could say that a just social order is one in which personal morality is not undermined by collective life or one in which we do not have to choose between our own self-preservation and that of others. The private manufacturer who wishes to pay his employees fair wages (enough for a decent standard of living) because their well-being matters to him stimulates creativity and personal responsibility for the end product because he knows what alienation means. He creates an environment where fulfilling interpersonal relations are possible because he sees his workers as fellow beings and chooses less polluting but more expensive production methods because he feels responsible for his biosphere and future generations. Yet, he will most probably be bankrupt after a few weeks because the real price of the product will be higher than the market price. He will be punished for not being productive and efficient enough. So even if we believe that modern societies cannot but be impersonal, technological, artefactual, and heartless, we must face the fact that this condition may well be dehumanizing us. In the next chapters, I will suggest ways in which we could possibly integrate the law of love and the dialogical principle into both corporate organizations and our political economy.

NOTES

1. Max Scheler, *On Feeling, Knowing, and Valuing: Selected Writings,* ed. Harold J. Bershady (Chicago and London: The University of Chicago Press, 1992), 159. Note that Scheler is here referring to the metaphysical idea of the primacy of love and not to the love commandment that can be found in the Hebrew bible.
2. Ibid.
3. Martha C. Nussbaum, *Love's Knowledge: Essays on Philosophy and Literature* (Oxford: Oxford University Press, 1990).
4. Arendt, *The Human Condition*, 52.
5. Jean-Claude Kaufmann, *The Curious History of Love*, trans. David Macey (Cambridge: Polity Press, 2011 [2009]), 48.
6. Ibid, 143.
7. Ibid, 154.
8. Ibid, 155.
9. Arendt, *The Human Condition*, 242.
10. Ibid, 243.
11. Scheler, *On Feeling, Knowing, and Valuing*, 158.
12. Kaufmann, *The Curious History of Love*, 13.
13. Buber, *Pointing the Way*, 221.
14. Kaufmann, *The Curious History of Love*, 11.
15. Niebuhr, *Love and Justice*, 112.
16. Geoffrey Holsclaw, *Society and Freedom, in Transcending Subjects: Augustine, Hegel, and Theology* (Chichester: John Wiley & Sons Ltd, 2016), 205.
17. Patrick Riley, *Leibniz' Universal Jurisprudence: Justice as the Charity of the Wise* (Cambridge, MA: Harvard University Press, 1996); Paul Tillich, *Love, Power and Justice* (Oxford: Oxford University Press, 1977); Adam Smith, *The Theory of Moral Sentiments* (Indianapolis: Liberty Fund, 1984), 86, 137, 175; Paul Ricoeur, *Amour et Justice* (Paris: Éditions Points, 2008 [1990]).
18. Mary T. Clark, "Augustine on Justice," *Revue d'Etudes Augustiniennes et Patristiques* 9, no. 1–2 (1963): 87–94.
19. Donald X. Burt, *Friendship and Society: An Introduction to Augustine's Practical Philosophy* (Grand Rapids, MI and Cambridge, UK: William B. Eerdmans Publishing Company, 1999), 4; Cf. Tillich, *Love, Power and Justice*, 25–26.
20. Scheler, *On Feeling, Knowing, and Valuing*, 156.

21. Scheler goes on to say that "all pantheism, from Spinoza to Hegel and Schopenhauer, has accepted this essentially false proposition." Ibid, 155.

22. Saint Augustine, *The City of God. Books VIII-XVI*, trans. Gerald G. Walsh and Grace Monahan (Washington, DC: Catholic University of America Press, 2008 [1952]), 289 (Book XII, chapter 22).

23. Ibid, 296 (Book XII, chapter 28).

24. Scheler, *On Feeling, Knowing, and Valuing*, 161.

25. Augustine, "Sermon 335C: On the Feast of a Martyr," in *Augustine: Political Writings*, eds. E.M. Atkins and R.J. Dodaro (Cambridge: Cambridge University Press, 2004), 54.

26. Ibid, 59.

27. Cicero, *On the Republic*, 52 (Book I, 51–52).

28. Saint Augustine, *The City of God. Books I-VII*, trans. Demetrius B Zema and Gerald Groveland Walsh (Washington, DC: Catholic University of America Press, 2008), 110 (Book II, chapter 21).

29. Cicero, *On the Republic*, 66 (Book II, 12).

30. The "rape" of the Sabine daughters is generally translated as their "abduction." There does not seem to be consensus on whether sexual abuse was involved.

31. Augustine, *The City of God. Books I-VII*, 97 (Book II, chapter 17).

32. It must be noted that pagans too belonged to the City of God. Sibyl, the prophetess, was one of them. All those who were against the worship of idols and all those who lived according to God's law "belonged to the spiritual Jerusalem." Augustine, *The City of God. Books XVII-XXII*, trans. Daniel J Honan, and Gerald Groveland Walsh (Washington, DC: Catholic University of America Press, 2008), 166 (Book XVIII, chapter 47).

33. Augustine, "Sermon 13: Christ, the Glory of Martyrs," in Augustine, *Commentary on the Lord's Sermon on the Mount*, 350.

34. Augustine, *The City of God. Books XVII-XXII*, 205 (Book XIX, chapter 6).

35. Niebuhr uses "egoism," "egotism," and "self-love" interchangeably. This is unfortunate and misleading. A more accurate terminology could have prevented criticisms from feminists, as I have argued elsewhere. See Roshnee Ossewaarde-Lowtoo, "Conquering Megalomania and Despair: A Niebuhrian Response to the Politico-Economic Impasse," *International Journal of Public Theology* 13, no. 3 (2019): 339–359, 342–343.

36. Reinhold Niebuhr, *Moral Man and Immoral Society: A Study in Ethics and Politics* (London: SCM Press Ltd, 1963), 84.

37. Reinhold Niebuhr, *An Interpretation of Christian Ethics* (New York: Meridian Books, 1956), 110.

38. Niebuhr, *Christianity and Power Politics*, 63.

39. Reinhold Niebuhr, *Christian Realism and Political Problems* (London: Faber and Faber, 1954), 43.

40. Niebuhr *An Interpretation of Christian Ethics*, 163.

41. Niebuhr, *Christianity and Power Politics*, 14.

42. Niebuhr, *Moral Man and Immoral Society*, 276–277.

43. Niebuhr, *Christian Realism and Political Problems*, 41.

44. Niebuhr, *Christianity and Power Politics*, 85–86.
45. Niebuhr, *An Interpretation of Christian Ethics*, 105.
46. Niebuhr, *Christian Realism and Political Problems*, 135.
47. In the next chapter, I will explain why "self-love" is a problematic term. Whenever I do use it, I consider it as reflecting the sole concern with one's own interests. There is no love, in the proper sense of the word, involved.
48. Niebuhr, *Moral Man and Immoral Society*, 47.
49. Niebuhr, *Faith and Politics*, 30.
50. Ibid, 30.
51. Niebuhr, *Moral Man and Immoral Society*, 57.
52. Niebuhr, *Christian Realism and Political Problems*, 155.
53. Niebuhr, *Moral Man and Immoral Society*, 265.
54. Cf. Abraham Heschel, *Man is Not Alone: A Philosophy of Religion* (New York: Farrar, Strauss & Giroux, 1951).
55. Niebuhr, *Christianity and Power Politics*, 2.
56. Niebuhr, *Faith and Politics*, 13.
57. Buber, *I and Thou*, 11.
58. Martin Buber, *A Believing Humanism: My Testament 1902-1965*, trans. M. Friedman (New Jersey and London: Humanities Press International, Inc., 1990), 119.
59. Ibid, 116; Buber, *I and Thou*, 35.
60. Martin Buber, *Between Man and Man*, trans. R. G. Smith (London: Kegan Paul, 1947), 20–21.
61. Martin Buber, *The Way of Man* (Oxford: Routledge, 1994), 32.
62. Ibid, 33.
63. Ibid.
64. Buber, *I and Thou*, 75.
65. Buber, *Between Man and Man*, 204.
66. Buber, *I and Thou*, 11.
67. Buber, *Between Man and Man*, 20–21.
68. Ibid.
69. Buber, *Pointing the Way*, 65–66; Buber, *Between Man and Man*, 98.
70. Buber, *Pointing the Way*, 111.
71. Osborne, *Eros Unveiled*, 49.
72. Ibid, 17.
73. Buber, *I and Thou*, 75.
74. Osborne, *Eros Unveiled*, 50.
75. Buber, *Pointing the Way*, 29.
76. Ibid.
77. Ibid, 29–30.
78. Ibid, 30.
79. Ibid, 109.
80. Niebuhr, *Christian Realism and Political Problems*, 145.
81. Buber, *The Way of Man*, 17.
82. Martin Buber and Maurice Friedman, "Interrogation of Martin Buber," in *Philosophical Interrogations: Interrogations of Martin Buber, John Wild, Jean Wahl,*

Brand Blanshard, Paul Weiss, Charles Hartshorne, Paul Tillich, eds. Sydney C. Rome and Beatrice K. Rome (New York: Holt, Rinehart and Winston, 1964), 79.

83. Ibid.

84. Ibid, 80.

85. Buber quoted in Maurice Friedman, *My Friendship with Martin Buber* (New York: Syracuse University Press, 2013), 102.

Chapter 3

Justice Begins with Oneself

FROM MINIMAL SELVES TO WHOLESOME SELVES

The idea that unified or well-ordered souls are the precondition for justice and, even more strongly, that justice consists in a unified soul is rarely present in modern discourses on justice and mainstream educational programs. It is true that violence and other forms of asocial behavior are commonly blamed on a wrong upbringing or "barbarism." Yet, socialization or training in civility is not exactly equivalent to the unity of the self. Moreover, justice is not just about civility and refraining from doing harm. As I have been arguing, it is about recognizing and bearing our responsibilities for strangers and is therefore about the expansion of our love. That expansion of our love, that is, the broadening of our loyalties is an important aspect of works inspired by Jewish, Christian, ancient and early modern humanist traditions. It thus also reappears in Rousseau's pedagogy, which is worth mentioning because of his avant la lettre phenomenology. Though the conception of that unity or wholeness does differ per tradition, with varying emphases on the passions and the body, it typically involves all human faculties, that is, the "whole" human being. Modern education, on the other hand, consists primarily in the training for the labor market. Parental education, more often than not, promotes the passions and ideas that are conducive to a "successful" life. Even an education that aims at enhancing human creativity does not adequately prepare persons for justice unless it fosters the sense of fellowship and responsibility. As Buber observes, the development of the "instinct of origination," which is directed to doing and not having, never becomes greed. However, as a creator, the person is a solitary being who does not enter dialogical life.[1]

The affirmation of otherness, implied by the norm of dialogue, should prevent possible misunderstandings evoked by the emphasis on "unity."

The unity or wholeness of the self should not be confused with some form of monism and the principle of oneness that I criticized earlier. The unity in question here is the unity of the self or soul and is not about sameness, uniformity, or order. Similarly, the unity of the self is not a one-off event or state of nirvana (or, bliss) that cannot be lost anymore. Instead, it is an ongoing, nonlinear process that is characterized by intermittent progress and regression. Perhaps, it is better to speak in terms of the *aspiration* to wholeness. The notion of the unity of the self is arguably a better alternative than the terminology "healthy identity" since the former captures both the coming-to-be of personhood and any nonobjectifiable permanent element that makes a person unique. This means that it is not only any eventual "core" or "center" in a person that distinguishes her from someone else. The ways in which she lives her life, relates to her world and fellow beings also make her who she becomes. The lifelong, tedious and somewhat mysterious process of the making of the self—in the world—tends to defy the categories of constructivism and essentialism. The unified self is also the antithesis of external ready-made identities that are endorsed in order to mask a fragmented selfand to deal with the chaos of such fragmentation.

By underscoring the need to unify the self, I am not denying the fragmentariness and complexity of life and the various "roles" that we have to play in our daily life. However, certain conflicting roles—and hence passions—might be a sign of something fundamentally wrong. For instance, isn't it remarkable that we adopt the buy low and sell high mentality, without regard to the needs of the other, as soon as we enter the economic "field" while still being loving parents, partners, and friends "outside" that field? So even if fragmentariness is inherent to human life, we may well be legitimizing unjust conditions by accepting certain (inner) conflicts as normal or inevitable. Being just with all one's soul in every single situation is extremely exacting, but it is the demand that follows from the law of love. The great character, according to Buber, is:

> One who by his actions and attitudes satisfies the claim of situations out of deep readiness to respond with his whole life, and in such a way that the sum of his actions and attitudes expresses at the same time the unity of his being in its willingness to accept responsibility [. . .] But the command inherent in a genuine norm never becomes a maxim and the fulfilment of it never a habit.[2]

We no longer find ourselves in the realm of deontological and virtue ethics. We are instead engaged in living our human lives as fully as possible as whole human beings in dialogic relations with others. The unity of the soul (like dialogic life) is not a luxury but is the precondition for wholesome human relations. Indeed, a fragmented self is not only an individual problem. Others suffer from our fragmented selves and from our unwillingness to examine the causes of such fragmentation. For example, the fragmentation required and caused by the game of the (fictive) homo economicus does not suddenly stop when we leave the economic realm, if we ever leave it at all. We are the same fragmented selves in our "noneconomic" relationships even if we try to play different roles.

Certain ideas regarding the formation of personhood and corresponding practices have therefore overshadowed the need to become whole, unified selves. Our culture itself has been generating what Lasch dubbed "the minimal self."[3] Minimal selves are too much preoccupied with (psychic) survival to be able to love. Injustice, I therefore argue, stems from too little care of the self and not so much from too much "self-love." I believe that the focus on "self-love" distracts us from the real issue, which is one of absent or insufficient love. In fact, the very term "self-love" is linguistically and psychologically quite incoherent since it suggests that I can direct my love to my self and therefore split myself into both subject and object. Loving, by definition, requires two. It would be more correct or much more in accordance with human experience to say that "self-love" refers to the incapacity to love, that is, to the incapacity to direct my attention, heart, and mind to someone else. Egoism and narcissism, both in very specific senses, are better terms to capture particular attitudes that involve extremely narrow loyalties, indifference to the needs of others, and the preference of our own interests above those of others. My conception of egoism here agrees with that of Scheler and with Rousseau's idea of amour-propre, which involves comparison, envy, pride, and vanity. More precisely, Rousseau notes that egoism (amour-propre) is "pride in great souls, vanity in petty ones."[4] According to Scheler,

> In "egoism" the given object of love is not my individual self, released from all social ties and thought of as merely a vessel for such supreme categories of value as those which find expression, for instance, in the concept of "salvation." Its object is simply myself, as one in competition with others, who thereupon simply "fails to observe" that others have any value. It is typical of egoism that it implies a *glance at other people* and their values and goods, and consists in just this "*failure to observe*" the claims engendered by these values.[5]

Egoism is more likely to prevail in democratic societies where we are stimulated to compare ourselves with each other. This is the ideal environment for the thriving of the feeling of inferiority. As Rousseau writes, "the sentiment of inferiority poisons everything. [. . .] One becomes preoccupied with what one does not have."[6] We are tormented by jealousy and discontentment.

Narcissism, on the other hand, is a much more passive state. I am here having recourse to Lasch's work on the culture of narcissism.[7] This latter terminology has been misunderstood. His critics, Lasch notes, have failed to grasp the loss of selfhood and the "inner emptiness" that are implied by narcissism. The characteristics of narcissism are those of a culture of survivalism: we feel too threatened and are too busy surviving to be concerned with others.[8] Lasch explains:

> The minimal or narcissistic self is, above all, a self uncertain of its own outlines, longing either to remake the world in its own image or to merge into its environment in blissful union. The current concern with 'identity' registers some of this difficulty in defining the boundaries of selfhood.[9]

Gilles Lipovetsky has critically re-appropriated Lasch's terminology and recast it into "neo-narcissism" in order to grasp the "dissolution of the Me," brought about by a culture that is allergic to effort, discipline, and self-mastery.[10] Narcissistic selves suffer from indifference and apathy and not so much from the despair predicted by Nietzsche. Narcissus is "fragilized" and "labile," frustrated at not being able to realize herself.[11] Even more recently, Anne Manne has taken up this theme in her *The Life of I: The New Culture of Narcissism* (2014).[12] Though she does not fully agree with Lasch's thinking (and does not seem to have grasped the full import of the lack of selfhood that Lasch emphasizes), she does acknowledge the effect of culture on personality. Anders Breivik, according to her, is a symptom of that culture. The "siege mentality" pointed out by Lasch has not lessened. On the contrary, "strategies of psychic survival" are overly visible today.[13] In order to counter this siege mentality, we must address both the external and "internal" conditions that fuel it. In the first case, we must make our immediate environments less threatening, both conceptually and practically. This is the subject of the next chapters. In the present chapter, I consider some ideas and practices that might help us to transcend tendencies toward egoism and narcissism.

THE WELL-ORDERED SOUL

I now wish to explore two approaches to the ordering of the soul, namely, a Platonic/Socratic version and one developed by Buber. The common and crucial element in both approaches consists in the idea that a unified soul is an absolute prerequisite for good interpersonal relationships and "works all of a piece."[14] A few years ago, there were debates as to whether a president is supposed to be "good." The short answer is no, quite surprisingly, since constitutions do not say much about the characters of the political representatives of a nation. The longer answer is that the political authority is expected to not abuse his power, to respect the law, and to subordinate his own personal ambitions (with regard to power and wealth, for instance) to the public interest of the nation. Similarly, business elites are not required to be "good," but they are expected to obey the law, keep their promises, and assume their corporate social responsibility. Sometimes, the "integrity" of political and business leaders is praised. Though "integrity" in these cases is not understood as the state of being "complete" or undivided—which is the original meaning of integrity—our current conceptions of the term do reflect its stronger sense. We admire people who are consistent in word and deed. They say what they mean and do what they say. They seem to be the same persons in different contexts and roles. They are trustworthy and we know what to expect from them even in dire situations. These persons can order and reconcile their inner conflicting commitments, time and again. Their wise decisions reflect their own inner wisdom. I think that we do expect our political and corporate elites to be "good" because we expect them to make the right choices. Such wisdom, as I will show, does depend on a unified self. The ordering process, however, is not the same in the two approaches that I here reconstruct.

In Plato's *Politeia*, we see that the ideal of the well-ordered soul and the ideal of the well-ordered city-state are connected. The *Politeia* is a utopia and thus no blueprint for the organization of societies. Individual freedom and personality, so important to us moderns, do not seem to matter in the ideal State as conceived by Plato. Given the fact that much has already been written on this topic and that I am now not concerned with the ideal political form, we can leave this thorny subject aside. Instead, I wish to consider the Socratic version of the well-ordered soul and the conceived link between inner order or peace, on the one hand, and interpersonal or even "inter-national" (inter-city) peace, on the other hand. The discussion starts with the question as to whether justice or injustice is more profitable. The common opinion, as articulated by Socrates' interlocutors, is that injustice is more profitable. Socrates tries to show that if being "profitable" is defined as being conducive to happiness, then justice is more profitable. It is noteworthy that he believes that his audience will be better able to grasp what inner, personal justice is if they understand what justice is between people in a city-state and between cities. Socrates asks whether a city can achieve anything if it is internally torn by discord: "tell me whether you think that a city or an army or bandits or thieves or any other group which sets about any unjust action together, could achieve anything if they wronged one another?"[15] In other words, for an (unjust) action to be effective, there need to be cooperation among the unjust, and there can be no cooperation if all want to harm each other. This leads Socrates to conclude that the unjust who can act together toward a common goal cannot be completely unjust.[16] A strong city-state could allegedly not have become strong without a minimum of justice.

Socrates' reasoning is problematic, to put it mildly. We know that it is possible for a nation of disciplined and dehumanized people to conquer another nation. The point that Socrates is trying to make is that wrongdoing leads to dissention, while "justice," in the narrow sense of not harming each other, fosters cooperation. This conception of justice as not harming the other is not only narrow, but more importantly, it does not tally with the Socratic/Platonic understanding of justice as the excellence of the soul. In other words, Socrates' attempt to understand inner, personal justice by drawing the analogy between the person and the city or a band of robbers is not very successful. Yet, it can be made more credible and fruitful by further qualifying the common action as good. That common end cannot be the petty theft of common thieves, the organized crime of the mafia, the coordinated actions of human traffickers, or the grand robberies of conquerors.[17] This further qualification is also necessary at the personal level. The divided person who is torn by conflicting values and passions can, of course, act and perhaps even act effectively if effective action means murdering or robbing someone. His actions are unjust and destructive. Good works, on the other hand, do require a unified soul. From the above, we may get the impression that justice is of value to society and not necessarily to the individual person. That would seem to confirm the common opinion that we are just out of fear of punishment, which Socrates is asked to refute. He does so by claiming that the person who possesses justice is blessed ("happy") because he is at peace with himself. The unjust person is torn by inner strife and is therefore his own enemy.

The person with the well-ordered soul is happy because his rational, appetitive, and spirited (in the sense of belonging to the *thymos*) faculties are ordered. Referring to the "three parts" of the soul, Socrates explains:

> A man does not allow the individual faculties within him to get involved in the functions of others, nor the parts of the soul to meddle with each other, but he puts what are really his own interests in good order, directs and disciplines himself, becomes a friend to himself and arranges those three elements together like, simply, the three defining notes of the scale, lower, upper and middle, and any others that happen to lie in between. He binds these all together and from many elements becomes in every respect a unity, temperate and harmonious; then and only then should he act, if he is having anything to do with the earning of money, or looking after his physical needs, or any business of the state, or his own private business arrangements: in every one of these he evaluates them and calls his activity as just and fair which preserves and helps to complete this state of affairs. The understanding which oversees this activity he calls wisdom, while the unjust action is that which would continually ruin all this, and the belief which oversees it, ignorance.[18]

Only the person whose soul is not torn by inner conflict should engage in economic and political activities. Even more ordinary activities require a well-ordered soul. In the above citation, we see that the end is further qualified as a creative end and not a destructive one (such as pillage or murder).

As noted above, Socrates draws the parallel between the ordering of the city-state and the ordering of the soul. According to this perspective, justice at the collective level requires that the three classes of the city-state, namely, the moneymaking (craftsman and wage earner), the auxiliary (military), and deliberative (guardian) classes mind their own businesses and do not transgress the boundaries of their classes.[19] The guardian class is the lover of wisdom and should thus also be the ruling class in society. The military class is a lover of success and honor, while the moneymaking class is a lover of profit.[20] The infamy of this caste system can distract us from seeing the intimate connection between the unity of the soul and justice. Moreover, as I already noted in the previous chapters, the "traditional" conception of justice as giving to all what is due to them according to their class or status is a lower form of justice than giving to all what is due to them by virtue of their humanity. In fact, it might not even be a lower form of justice at all but simply injustice. A "peaceful" societal order in which some members of humankind are considered to be born to serve others and are brought up with this belief is a just order if we believe that such a hierarchy is pre-given and eternal. It is unjust if we believe in the equal dignity of human beings and acknowledge the variety of all-too-human motives behind social stratifications. Such an order remains unjust even if it serves the material interests of a society. Wealth, peace, or military success is not necessarily a sign of justice. These observations also apply to modern social stratifications, which depend on concepts such as talents, merits, and IQ.

It is possible to abandon Socrates' (or Plato's) conception of justice at the collective level and retain the idea of the well-ordered soul as well as the insight that interpersonal conflicts reflect inner conflicts. In this ancient Greek model of the unification of the soul, the rational faculty is conceived as the governing force in the soul, to which the spirited faculty is subordinated and auxiliary. The right upbringing consists in nurturing the rational and spirited faculties so that they can control the appetitive part of the soul. This larger part of the soul "is naturally most greedy for material things." The two former faculties have the task of ensuring that the desires belonging to the latter faculty do not expand in such a way as to enslave the whole human soul and body.[21] Disorder thus arises when the rational faculty and the spirited faculty (from which the passions stem) are overwhelmed by the desires stemming from the appetitive faculty. The wrong upbringing can similarly lead to the "dominance of the spirited element [*thumoeidous*]" so that the love of victory and honor dominates the whole soul, blurring reason and fueling desires.[22] It is ironical that precisely this spirit of contentiousness and ambition has become a virtue today. Similarly, the idea that the appetitive faculty needs to be regulated has been lost. The Socratic/Platonic model of the unification of the soul can perhaps help us understand the need for balancing our different commitments and even attain some kind of balance. It may also deceive us into believing that we have achieved a well-ordered soul governed by a clairvoyant rational faculty that sees the right order of things. One of the main weaknesses of the ancient rationalist approach is its reliance on what has been referred to as a separative model of human nature in the previous chapters. The next model, on the other hand, contains an external "test," namely, the extent to which the person can assume responsibility for the world and address all beings and things as a Thou.

Another limitation of the previous approach lies in its portioning of the human soul into objective parts and in thereby failing to comprehend the human as a whole. Since the whole is greater than the sum of parts and encompasses inscrutable depths of the human soul, the person finds his deeper self by the "reversal of his whole being."[23] The human capacity to turn, to change direction and choose a different way toward our "destined being" is the joyful core of the Hasidic teaching as understood by Buber.[24] The Hasidic model of the unity of the soul is more comprehensive than the Socratic/Platonic model by including many more dimensions that are involved in the unification of the soul, ranging from the body to the world. The very understanding of the "soul" changes when we emphasize the whole being rather than a hierarchy of parts that constitute the human. The "soul," Buber points out, should not be misunderstood as referring to the most important part of the human. Instead, it is the whole being, body and spirit together. "The soul," he observes, "is not really united, unless all bodily energies, all the limbs of the body, are united."[25] Integrity consists in doing deeds with our whole being, including our physical being; it consists in saying things that we mean with our whole being, without hidden thoughts and feelings. In an even stronger sense, practices, which are physical, affect the unity of our self. They can foster it or undermine it. There are three important ways in which Buber's conception of the unity of the soul differs from the previous model. These are the ideas of the uniqueness of every soul, of his (her) vocation and, correspondingly, of his (her) destined being and of the embeddedness of the self in relationships with nature, other selves, and spiritual beings.[26]

"Every person born into this world," according to Buber, "represents something new, something that never existed before, something original and unique [. . .] called upon to fulfil his particularity in this world."[27] The embeddedness in the world should here be noted. The self achieves his (her) destined being in the world and discovers his (her) own particular way of redeeming that same world. The works done with our unified souls promote the redemption of the world, but they also lead to "a *steadier* unity" of our souls.[28] In other words, the practice of the good heals the world, others, and our own selves. Human souls are intricately connected to each other and to their world. They are even more intimately connected to the divine force in their depths. As Buber writes:

> The man with the divided, complicated, contradictory soul is not helpless: the core of his soul, the divine force in its depths, is capable of acting upon it, changing it, binding the conflicting forces together, amalgamating the diverging elements—is capable of unifying it. This unification must be accomplished *before* a man undertakes some unusual work. Only with a united soul will he be able to do it that it becomes not patchwork but work all of a piece. The Seer [in the story] thus reproaches the hasid with having embarked on his venture without first unifying his soul; unity of the soul can never be achieved in the middle of the work.[29]

This insistence on the necessity to unify our souls *before* taking important decisions and performing important tasks is fascinatingly similar to Socrates' emphasis that we should act only after having reached internal unity.

The care of the self is therefore not an excuse for some form of egocentrism and constant preoccupation with ourselves. It is the beginning of justice because we address the inner conflicts in ourselves that manifest themselves in external conflicts. The care of the self begins with the self but ends with the world and others. We owe it to our world and to others to undertake the tedious process of becoming whole and of starting all over again if we drift away from our destined being. Sounder economic and political systems and structures depend on the transformed souls of those who are willing to change things and accept changes. The "destined being" to which I have referred is not as esoteric or mystical as it may sound. We do not need special revelation or clairvoyance to discover it. As Buber points out,

> The environment which I feel to be the natural one, the situation which has been assigned to me as my fate, the things that happen to me day after day, the things that claim me day after day—these contain my essential task and such fulfilment of existence as is open to me.[30]

That is not to say that we are thrown back on our powers of discernment. The educator (parent, teacher, mentor, or friend) has the important task of helping young people find their own paths and keeping their desire to turn alive. Those of us who can no longer rely on such support are faced with the additional challenge of letting others into our lives and allowing them to guide us. Of course, such relationships are of a dialogical nature and, consequently, exclude all forms of manipulation and inequality. Especially those who hold positions of power are vulnerable to false and self-interested advice while they are in such dire need of the truth. The solution to this dilemma is to choose confidants from different milieus and associate with those who prefer truth to flattery.

AUGUSTINIAN REALISM AND THE SELF

In the previous chapter, I noted that Buber's conception of love is free from the theological complications that haunt the Christian version of love especially when it comes to the universal accessibility to divine love. We have seen that, for Buber, the divine force works in the depths of all human souls and does not restrict itself to the souls of those who have presumedly been "saved." In this regard, Buber remarks that while Christianity "makes each man's salvation his highest aim," according to Judaism, human souls are called to redeem God's Creation through their works so that it may become the Kingdom of God.[31] The motive here is not temporal or eternal happiness but is instead the love of the world. I believe that Buber's recast Hasidism is a much-needed corrective to some aspects of Christian thinking. However, these problematic tendencies (toward exclusivism, for instance) are especially to be found in theology and much less in Christian philosophical anthropology. Since I am here concerned with the self and its unity, theological controversies are not so relevant. I will thus now turn to Augustine's notion of the undivided heart and Niebuhr's updated and more sophisticated (in the positive sense of the term) Augustinian version of the self. However, the reader may wonder: what do those Christian accounts of the unity of the self add to what we have already seen above? As I have noted earlier, Augustine and later (hyper-)Augustinian traditions have played a decisive role in shaping our modern Western self-understanding. Certain aspects of these traditions are valuable because they reveal the inner contradictions of the self but also ways to surmount them. They should therefore be retrieved and kept. Ideas that foster individualism, anti-Semitism, Christian exclusivism, and the fear of the body must be either corrected or discarded.

Though Augustine may have wrongly generalized his own struggle with his sexual longings, his story of how he got delivered from "the chains of sexual desire" might help those who are in thrall to similar disorders.[32] He never really gives up the tendency to blame the body for the attachment to the material things of the world.[33] His way to deal with such attachment was a two-step program, namely, asceticism that was followed by temperance.

Asceticism helps to prepare the way for the unification of the self by temporarily protecting the soul from temptations. However, it is not equivalent to the unity of the soul, and it does not guarantee it. Envy and avarice—in the strong sense of the incapacity to be happy for someone else—are not exactly bodily.[34] We can imagine purely spiritual beings being envious and avaricious. Similarly, the role of the *libido dominandi* in disordered sexual desire has often enough been pointed out. The desire to possess and to dominate is hardly a purely bodily phenomenon. The more insightful Augustine saw that his "feelings of sexual desire" and other lusts followed from the "perversion of the will," that is, conflicting directions of his will.[35] Augustine blames the division of the heart on the incapacity to fully commit to what is truly good. He thus writes:

> So when eternity above delights us, and when pleasure in earthly prosperity keeps us down below, the soul is the same soul. It does not wish for one thing or the other with a complete will, and so ends up torn apart by its severe difficulties, as it prefers one thing for the sake of the truth, and yet because of ingrained habit fails to set the other thing aside.[36]

What helped to liberate Augustine from the shackles of lust was a greater love. The latter is not only the love for God but also the love of God for humankind. In other words, there is a mysterious mixture of human and divine love involved in the unity of self. Indeed, the worship of God in itself did not prove powerful enough to overcome Augustine's older attachments.[37] He writes: "For the law of sin is the brutality of habitual behavior: it drags and masters the mind even against its will, and it deserves this, because it sinks into such habits of its own free will."[38] Most of us will be able to recognize that all habits die hard, if they do die at all. What we learn from Augustine is that the unlearning of old habits is not simply a matter of choice, willpower, or even the love of higher goods. Divine empowerment is also involved. A moment of decision and thus choice is certainly involved. The redirection of our desire from lower goods to higher goods and the determination to persevere on the chosen path are prerequisites for defeating old habits. Augustine thus advises his audience: "Force your heart to think on divine things; urge it; compel it."[39] However, we see that it is not only a matter of right choice and focusing on what is truly important. The required strength to persevere and to unfailingly commit to the good despite external and internal obstacles is perhaps more often than not nearly inhuman. What finally liberated Augustine from the tentacles of his old habits is the fusion of divine love with his own desire for the good.[40] Good deeds are then no longer performed out of fear or desire for recognition (or praise). The simulation of goodness, on the other hand, reflects a divided heart and reinforces its division.[41] The peace of soul and purity of conscience that characterize the unified soul should not be regarded as permanent and indestructible. Vigilance remains vital.

Augustine is most probably not the first one to have conceived of a God who is intimately present in the depths of the human soul. He does, however, articulate the ways in which the divine force works in these depths and how human love is expanded through divine love. It is this "Augustinian formula for the leavening influence of a higher upon a lower loyalty or love" that Niebuhr appreciates in Augustine.[42] It prevents both defeatism and cynicism. In Niebuhr's later works, we therefore see a creative re-appropriation of the Augustinian legacy, more specifically, its biblical understanding of the human. Augustine's approach to the human, insofar as it distances itself from the neo-Platonic and mystic idea of undifferentiated being, does justice to the "mysteries of good and evil in human nature," which have been obscured by both naturalistic and idealistic philosophies.[43] Augustine, accordingly, would have been closer to his own thought if he had not claimed that there were two types of people dwelling in the earthly city—namely, those living according to man and the others living according to God—but had instead emphasized the two types of movements in every human soul—toward God and toward himself.[44] By becoming a Christian, one does not automatically get rid of the force of egotism and of the will-to-power. Even ascetic abbots were not free from the will-to-power, which did not express itself in greed, but in the "tyrannical rule over their monks."[45] Augustine's "interpretation of human selfhood," Niebuhr points out, "enables him to view the heights of human creativity and the depths of human destructiveness, which avoids the errors of moral sentimentality and cynicism."[46] Human lusts and ambitions are not irrational impulses but have to be understood against the background of human freedom and the corresponding capacity to transcend limits.

In his more biblical mood, Augustine understood that the mind was not the seat of virtue and the body could not be blamed for human depravities. Niebuhr contrasts Augustine's idea of the self to the classical dualism between body and mind. The self, for Augustine, refers to a mysterious identity, at least in some of his works. The body, the will, the mind, including memory and understanding, are aspects of the self, but they do not constitute the whole self. They belong to the self. The transcendence of the self is itself an essential dimension of the self. Therefore, it cannot be fitted into any kind of system, philosophical or (neuro)biological:

> The system obscures the height of his spirit, the uniqueness of his being, and the egoistic corruption of his freedom. That is why the dramatic-historical approach to human and divine reality validates itself despite the prestige of modern science. A scientific culture, despite its great achievements, exhibits a curious naïveté in surveying the human scene.[47]

The human is both free spirit who yearns for immortality and a mortal creature of nature. S(he) knows that s(he) is mortal and finite and yet constantly succumbs to the temptation of endowing his (her) partial views and achievements with an aura of universality (or immortality). Such constant occurrence reflects both the human need for spiritual security—unity and coherence—in the face of chaos and the will-to-power. Evil is therefore not simply the consequence of finiteness and/or bodiliness but quite inevitably follows from the human rebellion against his natural fate, his refusal to be content with his mortality and finitude. The perennial challenge of all human societies is therefore to prevent this existential struggle from turning into the will-to-power.

Following Augustine, Niebuhr maintains that in prophetic religion wickedness is not the result of the weakness, limitation or imperfection that belongs to a finite being but stems from the corruption of the will.[48] This means that despite the intellectual capacity to envisage the highest goods, the moral agent chooses the lesser good. In other words, reason is not that which determines the goals or the direction of commitments. It is instead the instrument of the self and his (her) commitments, which can be narrow or broad. Evil therefore does not become less with the progress of reason and civilization. In fact, Niebuhr notes that "the possibilities of evil grow with the development of the very freedom and power which were supposed to emancipate man."[49] This means that virtue is not simply the fruit of reason, and reason is not the guarantee for virtue. Old and modern rationalisms overlook the fact that intelligence can strengthen egoistic impulses and create order at a lower level (family or nation), which then becomes the source of anarchy at a higher level (imperialism).[50] That said, though natural impulses (sympathy and pity, for instance) are not inherently bad and, on the contrary, can be the source of a healthy will, Christian (prophetic) thinking, unlike Romanticism, appraises the social impulses critically. As Niebuhr notes,

> [The will] is neither the total personality nor yet the rational element in personality. It is the total organized personality moving against the recalcitrant elements in the self. The will implies a cleavage in the self but not a cleavage, primarily between reason and impulse. The will is a rational organization of impulse. Consequently, the Christian ideal of a loving will does not exclude the impulses and emotions in nature through which the self is organically related to other life.[51]

Hence, differently from Nygren and Luther, Niebuhr does not conceive of an absolute contradiction between *agape* and natural human love such as *eros* and *philia*.

The love commandment reveals the cleavage in the self: the self is not able to love his neighbor as himself. Of course, this reasoning only makes sense to those who have not naturalized and normalized the fact that we are unwilling (or, incapable) to put the interests of others on par with ours. Niebuhr writes:

> The liberal part of our culture thought that the Christian idea of the sinfulness of all men was outmoded. In its place it put the idea of a harmless egotism, rendered innocuous either by a prudent self-interest or by a balance of all social forces which would transmute the selfishness of all into a higher social harmony. The vanity of that idea was proved by the ever more dynamic disproportions of power in our society and the ever greater destruction of community in a technical society.[52]

The "ideal of love," according to Niebuhr, "is thus first a commandment which appeals to the will."[53] The love commandment demands from the self that he transcends his internal contradictions and love with his whole self. In fact, "all moral demands are demands of unity," Niebuhr notes, since "life must not be lived at cross-purposes. The self must establish an inner unity of impulses and desires and it must relate itself harmoniously to other selves and other unities."[54] Yet, unlike naturalistic ethic, Christian (prophetic) ethic does not simply accept egoism as an unchangeable, harmless fact. The religious ethic does not presume the automatic harmony of interests and a providentially pre-established order that is not affected by human egoism. Instead, the religious ethic demands, from a naturalistic perspective, an inhuman feat. In a strong sense, such unity is indeed an inhuman achievement since divine love is also involved in the becoming of the unified self.

So, what does the above account of the unity of the self imply for those of us who are not, or are no longer, committed to some form of Christianity? Ought we to give up the aspiration to the unity of the self and hence the idea of putting the needs of others (strangers) on par with ours? Of course, we could reply that the whole idea of the ontological dependence of our love on an extra-human love is nonsensical and a sign of our voluntary and cowardly self-inflicted tutelage. Such a response is to be expected if Taylor is correct in saying that our Western culture is characterized by the (ethical) narrative of our "coming of age," that is, of us moderns having had the courage to discard old illusions and to accept the "truth" that we have only ourselves to rely on.[55] The significant feature of this possible response or narrative is not so much the rejection of the presupposition of a divine love that permeates the world but rather the repudiation of the idea of dependence and hence of the idea that the highest human goal is love and fellowship. In other words, the clash here is not between "belief" and "unbelief," but it is one between different self-understandings and different conceptions of the highest goals of human existence. If we do consider love as the highest goal of human existence, we cannot but accept our dependence on others and the uncertainty that corresponds to such dependence. But suppose we do accept this ideal of love but do not see the point of assuming an extra-human love? My reply here is that we often implicitly do experience love as a causal power that enables us to surmount all kinds of obstacles. We rarely congratulate ourselves for such a feat. That love is both "ours" and more than ours. It is this latter mysterious reality of love that is captured by the religious imagery of an extra-human love working in the depths of the human soul. As Jean-François Lyotard so aptly writes, "Augustine was the first, with Paul, to reveal that inner share of the me with this Other who, in him, is more profound than him. More profound in that the me cannot understand it."[56] Religious language tries to articulate the human experience of inner contradictions, the human struggle to become whole and the inexplicable sources of empowerment during this journey. Whether we wish to use that language is really up to us. That language did not create the reality that it tries to express.

AN ACTIVE CONSCIENCE

The experience of inner struggles, the recognition of inner contradictions, and the willingness to explore the causes of the fragmentation of the self presume an active conscience, as opposed to a dormant conscience. Yet, the chasm between, on the one hand, the knowledge of what is just and good and actual practices, on the other hand may make us doubt the very existence of the "conscience" praised by so many. The trade in arms is not deterred by the knowledge regarding their uses in the annihilation of whole peoples. The despotism of regimes does not hinder business transactions. Tycoons are helped by lawyers and other financial advisors to evade taxes. Of course, such "money management" is not called evasion or fraud. We may wonder whether all those involved in such exploitative and dehumanizing activities experience pangs of conscience, consider themselves unjust or for that matter think in terms of justice at all. After all, it is not so difficult to redefine "justice" so that current practices are justified. In chapter one, I referred to Grotius' reconceptualization of justice so that the latter includes promoting one's own interests and seizing opportunities. There are thus many ways to placate our consciences. As John Gray critically points out, "morality tells us that conscience may not be heard—but that it speaks always against cruelty and injustice. In fact conscience blesses cruelty and injustice—so long as their victims can be quietly buried."[57] This is not completely a cynical remark. As Arendt once observed, the conscience of Eichmann spoke the "respectable voice" of the "respectable society" around him.[58] She tried to understand how someone (Eichmann) could be a good family man, have no hate for the Jews and still murder them. We can similarly try to understand how corporate leaders, politicians, and lawyers, for instance, can be committed to their families and friends and, at the same time, destroy the lives of others without hating them. Once we understand how and why consciences are distorted and numbed, we can find ways to prevent the slumber of our consciences.

The fact that our conscience is fragile is no reason to deny its existence. Love is also fragile, but most of us are unwilling to conclude that it is an illusion. Our human bodies are fragile, but they are very much part of our selves. The sublimity of conscience is eloquently praised by Rousseau. Very much in line with certain strands of Stoic, Jewish, and Christian thoughts, he considers conscience as the defining characteristic of humans. This sets him apart from rationalists who perceive reason as that which distinguishes humans from animals. Conscience, for him, is a divine voice, as it is in the aforementioned traditions. He thus writes:

> Conscience, conscience, divine instinct, immortal and celestial voice, assured guide of an ignorant and limited but intelligent and free being; infallible judge of the good and evil, sublime emanation of the eternal substance, which renders man like the Gods; only you constitute the excellence of my nature. Without you, I do not feel anything in me that elevates me above the beasts.[59]

Conscience is that which judges us and reproaches us for our wrongdoing or for our indifference. It also protects us from the deceptions of our reason. However, it is dependent on both reason and the heart, and as Rousseau emphasizes, on our sensitivity to beauty. Conscience must be cultivated and is thus not simply "in us," awaiting to be discovered. The infant, according to Rousseau, has no conscience. The latter develops as we learn to see our place in the world, our relations to others and acquire the ideas of propriety and justice. We learn to discern order and beauty. Conscience prompts us to love that order and beauty, the law and justice.[60] Conscience is no "infallible judge of good and evil," at least, not necessarily and automatically. Its dependence on a clearsighted reason and a humane heart also constitutes its "weakness." We see that conscience can love justice and beauty only if our reason and heart have not been corrupted.

Giving up on conscience is no option because that would be equivalent to allowing the "demonic" or the "antihuman" in us to win.[61] That would mean giving up responsibility. The fact that we are failing to respond to our responsibilities is already a sign that there is something terribly wrong with our consciences. Heschel saw the sickness of his age as "the failure of conscience rather than the failure of nerve. Our conscience is not the same. Stultified by its own bankruptcy, [. . .] it becomes subject to automation."[62]

For Buber, this failure of conscience means that we are no longer listening to the call of the "being which is not I."[63] The Israelites, according to Buber, survived their trial in the desert without turning into monsters because "Thou shalt not" never faded from their hearts and minds.[64] They did not forget that they were accountable to someone other than themselves. In their case, that was God. The "nonbelievers" among us can consider ourselves to be accountable to other beings, nature, a "cosmic order," or something indefinable. We again see that the sense of responsibility toward strangers and other beings—and in general, the whole planet—depends on whether we can see ourselves substantially ("thickly") related to them. This means that the voice of conscience is easily smothered when we deny or do not see that connection. To complicate things even more, it is indeed true that such an ontological relationship cannot be "seen" since it is not empirically observable. It can be imagined, but there is no compelling reason to imagine it unless we have somehow experienced it. In rare moments of exceptional insight, we may indeed catch a glimpse of the organic unity connecting us to everything and everyone in this world. Religious and philosophical traditions try to articulate that intuition. The latter, however, must be lived out in order to become real.

We may be aware of our responsibility toward our fellow beings in solitude and yet "forget" it when we play the foul game in the world. This is the frightening conclusion that Rousseau draws. This is also what Arendt suggests when she notes that the Eichmann and the Nuremberg trials reveal an evil that is committed without the distinction between wrong and right, between evil and good, because this very distinction is no longer clear or, even worse, has been reversed. What used to be wrong is now seen as the right thing to do, whereby "right" is that which is in accordance with prevailing laws. Individual consciences, if any, are smothered. Such a smothering of individual consciences seems to be taking place when corporate and political elites directly and indirectly destroy other peoples' lives through their actions and nonactions. It helps that they feel no bond with those people (who are often inhabitants of poorer countries where the rule of law is virtually nonexistent). In fact, there might even be contempt for the barbarians who have not been able to establish a minimum of civilization. The "enlightened" powerful can legitimize their actions and nonactions by pointing to the absence of democratic structures while they themselves benefit from such chaos. In fact, they, similarly to the old colonialists, often make deals with corrupt local leaders. The prevalence of chaos makes it easier for us to evade our responsibility. Since there are no laws, they cannot be transgressed. Moreover, if prevailing sociopolitical conditions are already so rotten, we cannot change them, and more importantly, it is not our task to change them. In these cases, it cannot be wrong to reap some benefits. These few examples illustrate what Rousseau called the sophisms of our reason.

They help to ease our consciences. An even more dangerous phenomenon is the political endorsement of business enterprises (multinationals), which results in the image that they act in the national interests of the country of origin. Since their activities are conceived as sources of wealth for a nation, the harm that is done to other peoples in this quest for wealth is more easily ignored.

Conscience is "shy and fearful."[65] Its voice is stifled in a society where "every man wants the entire universe, making them enemies of each other" and where the concern with commerce and money has become overriding.[66] Note that these are also the desires that undermine the unity of the self. In other words, a developed and active conscience belongs to a unified self. An active conscience therefore depends on whether we have been able to find our own selves and keep them unified in the world. Rousseau thus advises those who are immersed in worldly activities to regularly have recourse to retreats. In doing so, we leave the realm of competition and relearn to love our fellow beings. Writing to a so-called high society friend, he suggests that she devotes two to three days a month to the "most important matter" of all matters, which is solitude.[67] The capacity to be alone with oneself without being bored must be cultivated. Rousseau recommends the countryside, to be preferred to Paris, because "solitariness in a city is always depressing," while the countryside is more conducive to contemplation.[68] The "countryside" that he has in mind is a lively one, as opposed to desolate vast lands. It is marked by a luxuriant nature with which we can converse and that we can admire. In such an environment, our souls and hence our consciences are liberated from their numbness. It will soon become clear that Rousseau is not advocating complete seclusion. Solitude is also the precondition for introspection, that is, an exploration of our inner depths. More specifically, such inner exploration consists in questioning our motives and uncovering our even deeper motives, of which we may not even be aware. Introspection is one of the most effective manners in which we can activate our conscience and prevent it from being the mere internalization of the dominant culture and our unreasonable desires.

Introspection thus also aims at unveiling the clash between desires within ourselves. I would like to refer to such a critical introspection as reflexivity. Reflexivity makes us understand why we are attracted to certain goods (individual freedom and wealth, for instance). It sheds critical light on what we take for granted and consider being the only possibility. Is our notion of greatness truly great? Is what we consider the most important in our lives truly so? At the same time, reflexivity may make us aware of other latent desires, such as the desire for peace and the warmth of human intimacy. While reviewing our lives, we may stumble onto unfulfilled needs. We may also realize that we do not admire anything and that awe is an experience unknown to us. Such a discovery is rare. Buber thus notes:

> Most of us achieve only at rare moments a clear realization of the fact that they have never tasted the fulfilment of existence, that their life does not participate in true, fulfilled existence, that, as it were, it passed true existence by. We nevertheless feel the deficiency at every moment, and in some measure strive to find—somewhere—what we are seeking.[69]

Reflexivity is a tedious and confronting exercise. It is thus to be expected that we may be tempted to avoid such an undesirable disruption of our daily lives.

If I am "happy" with my life, why should I bother to examine it? It is therefore realistic to assume that such a review of our lives is incited by a form of discontent. That discontent helps to pop the bubble of self-delusion. Eichmann did not experience such discontent, and this is why he never questioned his practices. He had a clear conscience. Persons who have sold their souls to their parties, nations, and business and religious corporations are not easily moved. Their consciences do not bother them. The educator, according to Buber, has the important task of arousing that salutary discontent and keeping the pain of unfulfillment alive. She "can help the feeling that something is lacking to grow into the clarity of consciousness and into the force of desire. He can awaken in young people the courage to shoulder life again."[70] What about the not-so-young among us, who do not have an educator to guide them? How can the desire to seek full existence and to accept the responsibility for the world be awakened in City and Wall Street workers, the business magnate, politician, civil servant, or simply the administrative assistant? Let me here make one suggestion. As I noted earlier, we are not inclined to examine our lives if we are "satisfied." We may also be so taken up by our routines that we do not have the time to do so. Until we are overwhelmed by an extreme weariness and nausea at the inhumane automatism of our gestures. Such a moment, Albert Camus points out, "inaugurates the movement of consciousness."[71] That moment is decisive. We can go back to the same old routine or we can choose to change things. We can also choose to end it all through suicide. It might therefore be wise to not make reflexivity solely and purely an individual pursuit but to instead integrate it into professional educational programs as well as political and professional careers.

THE CARING SELF

The emphasis on the importance of solitude for the constitution of the self should not overshadow the fact that the self becomes a fully-fledged self in fellowship with other selves. Both solitude and this fellowship are undermined in contexts where productivity is the highest good. A twenty-four-hour economy reflects the utter contempt for human souls. We are admittedly constantly interacting with others, but this is often in virtual reality. Such interaction does not allow for the substantial, bodily relationships that characterize human fellowship. It could be concluded that the "quality" of selves and hence of individual consciences depends on the quality or "thickness" of our relationships and the extent to which we have fully lived and examined our lives. In this regard, it is noteworthy that Arendt blamed Eichmann's horrendous deeds on his "remoteness from reality," which she referred to as "thoughtlessness."[72] Of course, she did not mean that he was stupid. He was clever enough to organize the deportation of millions of victims to the gas chambers. His inability to think consisted in his inability to "think from the standpoint of somebody else."[73] Such a conception of thinking is also reflected in Aretha Franklin's song *Think*. Genuine thinking is dependent on compassion and empathy, that is, on the capacity to understand and feel from the perspective of the other. Imagination, in this respect, is not enough. Instead, we must get to know others who are not part of our immediate circles and, through genuine human encounters, experience something of that invisible bond that relates us to them. These genuine human encounters necessitate not only the appropriate urban and rural planning (in terms of buildings, residential areas, meeting places, and schools that foster such encounters) but also an attitude of care and attention.

Socioeconomic and ideological barriers and the corresponding separative architecture thwart genuine human encounters. Paradoxically enough, these barriers do not seem to have become weaker in our so-called democratic societies. This is the reason why Rousseau's practical guidance with respect to transcending the gap between different classes can still be useful to us today. Let me go back to his letter to his high society friend. He does not limit himself to recommending a retreat to the countryside, but he also goes into detail about how she should spend her days there. Clearly aware of the corrupting effects of being constantly served, Rousseau emphatically advises his friend to leave behind her attendants and servants. She is encouraged to follow the rhymes of nature and of the people. She is to become a "woman of the fields" as far as her sleeping and eating habits are concerned.[74] In her free time, she should take care of the sick, the poor, and the oppressed, not only financially but especially by giving them her attention, time, and physical care. Rousseau foresees that her friend, given her own habitual privileged milieu, will be put off by dirty houses, the roughness of the "common people," and all other features of poverty. Note here that Rousseau is certainly not idealizing country life. He therefore tells her to say to herself that she is their sister. "Humanity," Rousseau assures her, "will triumph over repulsion."[75] She will learn to forgive the lies and vices of the people as she realizes that she herself is not exempt from lies and vices, which may well be worse because they are hidden behind a polite mask. Rousseau's emphasis on the *physical*, that is, *bodily* involvement with those from a different milieu must be highlighted. Fellowship is about living together and sharing the burdens and not only about financial or emotional support. We may be able to overcome our repulsion and other obstacles if our interaction with people who are very different from us—or, who appear to be so different from us—is accompanied by what Simone Weil dubbed "watchful attention."[76] Such active form of attention may help us to see that "humanity" in the other.

Quite unsurprisingly, the more "intellectual" and "professional" layers of societies are at a higher risk of being denied the experience of fellowship because they are the most alienated from physical and thus bodily existence. In this regard, Lasch judiciously writes:

> Part of the trouble, I would add, is that we have lost our respect for honest manual labor. We think of 'creative' work as a series of abstract mental operations performed in an office, preferably with the aid of computers, not as the production of food, shelter, and other necessities. The thinking classes are fatally removed from the physical side of life—hence their feeble attempt to compensate by embracing a strenuous regimen of gratuitous exercise. Their only relation to productive labor is that of consumers. They have no experience of making anything substantial or enduring.[77]

We may be tempted to discard this observation as the romanticizing of primitive forms of labor (and life). However, whenever we do disagree with the above analysis, we must be wary of avoiding two mistakes. One is to think that we must all become bourgeois and thus occupy bourgeois professions. That seems to be the firm conviction of McCloskey, who consistently expresses her contempt for anyone who does not embrace the bourgeois ideal. As she writes: "A peasant prostrates himself before the gods; an aristocrat curses them; a priest organizes their worship. The bourgeois [Abraham] argues with his God and makes a little deal. I can get it for you wholesale."[78] The disdain for, or low valuation of, manual labor and physical caregiving is reflected in low wages or no wages at all, as in the case of women who are still primary caregivers and still do most household chores. The second mistake consists in disregarding the mediating role that the body and bodily activities play in our experience and knowledge of reality. Both the possibilities and limits of human life are revealed in our bodily existence. The recognition of these limits, as I have implied and will be showing in the next chapter, is the precondition for justice and peace and hence for true human happiness.

NOTES

1. Buber, *Between Man and Man*, 87.
2. Ibid, 114.

3. Christopher Lasch, *The Minimal Self: Psychic Survival in Troubled Times* (London: Pan Books, 1984), 57.

4. Jean-Jacques Rousseau, "Émile ou de l'éducation," in *Œuvres complètes de Jean-Jacques Rousseau IV*, eds. Bernard Gagnebin and Marcel Raymond (Paris: Editions Gallimard, 1969), 494. All translations are the author's.

5. Scheler, *On Feeling, Knowing, and Valuing*, 73. Italics are in the original text.

6. Jean-Jacques Rousseau, "Rousseau Juge de Jean-Jacques-Dialogues," in *Œuvres complètes de Jean-Jacques Rousseau I*, eds. Bernard Gagnebin and Marcel Raymond (Paris: Editions Gallimard, 1959), 806; Cf. Alfred Adler, "The Feeling of Inferiority and the Striving for Recognition," trans. Walter Béran Wolfe, *Journal of the Royal Society of Medicine* 20, no. 12 (1927): 1881–1886; Cf. Alfred Adler, *Understanding Human Nature* (New York: Greenberg Publisher, 1946), 75.

7. Christopher Lasch, *The Culture of Narcissism: American Life in an Age of Diminishing Expectations* (New York: W.W. Norton, 1978); Lasch, *The Minimal Self.*

8. Lasch, *The Minimal Self*, 57.

9. Ibid, 19.

10. Gilles Lipovetsky, *L'ère du vide: essais sur l'individualisme contemporain* (Paris: Gallimard, 1983), 63.

11. Gilles Lipovetsky and Bertrand Richard, *La société de déception* (Paris: Textuel, 2006), 27.

12. Anne Manne, *The Life of I: The New Culture of Narcissism* (Melbourne University Press, 2014).

13. Lasch, *The Minimal Self*, 18–19.

14. Buber, *The Way of Man*, 16.

15. Plato, *Republic, Volume I: Books 1-5*, edited and translated by Christopher Emlyn-Jones and William Preddy (Cambridge, MA: Harvard University Press, 2013), 103 (Book I).

16. Ibid, 109. Centuries later, Adam Smith quite similarly remarks that "if there is any society among robbers and murderers, they must at least, according to the trite observation, abstain from robbing and murdering one another." Smith, *The Theory of Moral Sentiments*, 86.

17. The legendary conversation between Alexander the Great and the pirate Diomedes suggests that emperors are pirates or robbers on a large scale.

18. Plato, *Republic, Volume I*, 435 (Book IV).

19. Ibid, 425.

20. Plato, *Republic, Volume II: Books 6-10.* Edited and translated by Christopher Emlyn-Jones and William Preddy (Cambridge, MA: Harvard University Press, 2013), 347 (Book IX).

21. Plato, *Republic, Volume I*, 429 (Book IV).

22. Plato, *Republic, Volume II,* 223 (Book VII).

23. Buber, *The Way of Man*, 25.

24. Buber, *I and Thou*, 42.

25. Buber, *The Way of Man*, 18.

26. Buber, *I and Thou*, 70.

27. Buber, *The Way of Man*, 9.
28. Ibid, 17. Italics in original text.
29. Ibid, 16.
30. Ibid, 31.
31. Ibid, 26.
32. Aurelius Augustine, *Confessions*. Vol. I, Books 1–8. Edited and translated by Carolyn J.-B. Hammond (Cambridge, MA: Harvard University Press, 2014), 379 (Book VIII).
33. Ibid, 159 (Book IV).
34. Cf. Adler, *Understanding Human Nature*, 227.
35. Augustine, *Confessions I*, 373, 375 (Book VIII).
36. Ibid, 403.
37. Ibid, 375.
38. Ibid, 377, 379.
39. Augustine, "Sermon 53: On the Beatitudes (Matt. 3.5-8)," in Augustine, *Commentary on the Lord's Sermon on the Mount*, 221.
40. Referring to Cicero as an exemplary linguist, Augustine notes that there is no reason for not using the verbs to "desire" and to "will" interchangeably. He thus writes: "Moreover, even in secular literature these verbs are used just as indiscriminately. For example, Cicero, who was never at a loss for the right word, says: 'I desire, gentlemen of the Senate, to be merciful.' Now if Cicero can use desire in a good sense, what precisionist has any right to say that Cicero should not have said 'I desire,' but 'I will?'" Augustine, *The City of God. Books VIII-XVI*, 364 (Book XIV, chapter 8). This is not only a linguistic matter, of course. Augustine is rehabilitating the goodness of desire and emotions such as fear and sorrow, refuting the Stoic theory that the wise man does not desire but only wills and does not fear and feel sorrow. The direction of the will (that is, our desire or love) can be good or bad, and this determines the goodness or wickedness of our passions.
41. Augustine, "Commentary on the Lord's Sermon on the Mount," 110 (Book II).
42. Niebuhr, *Christian Realism and Political Problems*, 129.
43. Ibid, 100.
44. Ibid, 131.
45. Niebuhr, *Christianity and Power Politics*, 148.
46. Niebuhr, *Christian Realism and Political Problems*, 12.
47. Ibid, 100.
48. Niebuhr, *An Interpretation of Christian Ethics*, 75.
49. Niebuhr, *Christian Realism and Political Problems*, 103.
50. Niebuhr, *An Interpretation of Christian Ethics*, 89.
51. Ibid, 188–189.
52. Niebuhr, *Christian Realism and Political Problems*, 102–103.
53. Niebuhr, *An Interpretation of Christian Ethics*, 188.
54. Ibid, 45.
55. Cf. Taylor, *A Secular Age*, 574–575.
56. Jean-François Lyotard, *Moralités Postmodernes* (Paris: Galilée, 1993), 182–183.

57. John Gray, *Straw Dogs: Thoughts on Humans and Other Animals* (London: Granta Books, 2002), 97.

58. Hannah Arendt, *Eichmann in Jerusalem: A Report on the Banality of Evil* (London: Penguin Books, 2006), 126.

59. Rousseau, "Lettres morales," *Œuvres complètes de Jean-Jacques Rousseau IV*, 1111.

60. It is noteworthy that both Adam Smith and Immanuel Kant, very much in line with the Stoic tradition, also believed in such an inner judge in all humans. This belief or assumption is an integral part of their moral theories.

61. Heschel, *Who is Man?*, 101; Buber, *A Believing Humanism*, 216.

62. Heschel, *Who is Man?*, 15.

63. Buber, *Between Man and Man*, 166.

64. Ibid, 109.

65. Rousseau, "Lettres morales," 1112.

66. Rousseau, "Lettre à Christophe de Beaumont," *Œuvres complètes de Jean-Jacques Rousseau IV*, 937.

67. Rousseau, "Lettres morales," 1115.

68. Ibid.

69. Buber, *The Way of Man*, 30.

70. Buber, *Between Man and Man*, 115.

71. Albert Camus, *Le mythe de Sisyphe: Essai sur l'absurde* (Paris: Gallimard, 1942), 27.

72. Arendt, *Eichmann in Jerusalem*, 288.

73. Ibid, 49.

74. Rousseau, "Lettres morales," 1118.

75. Ibid, 1115.

76. Weil, *Attente de Dieu*, 93. All translations are the author's.

77. Lasch, *The Revolt of the Elites*, 20.

78. Deirdre N. McCloskey, *The Bourgeois Virtues: Ethics for an Age of Commerce* (University of Chicago Press, 2006), 501.

Chapter 4

Reconciling Utility and Justice

THE PERENNIAL CONFLICT BETWEEN UTILITY AND JUSTICE

As I noted in the introduction, it would be terribly one-sided to blame injustice solely on our personal incapacity to transcend the fragmentation of ourselves. Certain features of our culture foster the indifference to (in)justice and therefore undermine our own aspirations to justice. In the present chapter, I would like to focus on the conceptual and practical preference for utility over justice. The conceptual prioritization of utility over justice is expressed in the neutralization of what used to be considered vices so that the unrestrained desire for material gain and prestige becomes legitimate. Indeed, how can these desires be foul if they make most of us and a country rich? Conversely, our forebears were simply wrong to think that humility and abstinence were virtues. Hence, Grotius, as I pointed out in chapter one, observes that the failure to exploit opportunities to enrich ourselves is a sin, that is, foul. Grotius' justification of the seizure of the Portuguese ship Santa Catarina is a magnificent illustration of the modern bourgeois morality. At the practical level, the reversal of traditional morality and hence injustice are sanctioned and reinforced by policies that favor more markets and more "freedom" for market players. To realize the dehumanizing nature of this morality and corresponding practices, I believe that we must regain some notion of the perennial conflict between utility and justice and understand why foul was never fair and cannot be fair. To this end, I here consider a few relevant passages in Plato's *Politeia* and Cicero's *De Re Publica*.

The idea that injustice pays is not new or modern. Similarly, doubt regarding the very meaning and possibility of justice must have been quite common in the ancient world, to judge from Plato's and Cicero's dialogues. In Plato's

Politeia, Thrasymachus claims that justice is determined by the strongest and is therefore nothing other than the advantage of the latter.[1] Thrasymachus thinks that Socrates is wrong to believe that those who occupy positions of responsibility act on behalf and for the benefit of their subjects. He quite persuasively argues that whenever people are in such positions, they act for their own benefits and, in fact, make use of those they are in charge of to their own personal ends.[2] Thrasymachus accuses Socrates of being out of touch with reality and thus not understanding that the just promote the happiness of those whom they serve to their own detriment. Whenever people are just, they are just out of fear. They are afraid of punishments; or they are just for the sake of honors and gifts.[3] This, of course, does not hold for Socrates, but he is far too naïve. The latter is challenged to defend justice as good in itself. Thrasymachus addresses himself to Socrates:

> You must look at the matter, my most simpleminded Socrates, thus: that the just man everywhere comes off worse than the unjust. To begin with, in business relations, wherever such a person collaborates with another such, nowhere would you find, when the association is concluded, that the just person has come off better than the unjust but worse. Secondly, in dealings with the city, when there are taxes to be paid, the just person contributes more and the unjust less out of equal resources, and when there are pay-outs the latter gains much, but the former nothing.[4]

Thrasymachus' observation is quite correct and not outdated at all. He is not even being cynical but is rather a realist. The financial gains of tax evasions or toxic dumping, for instance, cannot be denied. The outcomes of unjust practices, which are often sugar-coated in such a way that they become legal and even good, are profitable.

In Cicero's *De Re Publica*, Philus is asked to defend injustice as being more profitable than justice, both at interpersonal and collective levels. Many pages of that dialogue are missing in the various editions of that work, while some of them contain fragments quoted by Lactantius in his *Divine Institutes* (*institutiones divinae*) and fragments whose origin is uncertain. Augustine's comments also give us an idea of what may have been present in the original texts.[5] The conflict between the useful and virtue is illustrated when the Romans are referred to as the "most just of human beings," who, however, "do not permit the Transalpine nations to grow olive and vine, so that [their] olive groves and [their] vineyards will be worth more."[6] They may be acting "prudently," for the interests of their homeland, but they are not acting justly. Justice requires that they consider the interests of other nations on par with their own. But that does not seem to be possible without "losses." The origin of this fragment is uncertain. Similarly, in some other fragments (whose sources are either from Lactantius or simply unknown), Philus is reported to have illustrated his argument (that injustice might well be more profitable) with real life dilemmas, whereby individuals must choose between gain and survival, on the one hand, and deceiving and harming others, on the other.[7]

According to one story, two men have survived a shipwreck but have only one piece of floating wood to save one of them. Should the strongest of them seize that board and let the other man perish? Or suppose that both are of equal strength: should the one man allow his board to be snatched from him without fighting back? Though it is natural and prudent to save one's skin and foolish to allow oneself to be either beaten up or not to make use of one's natural advantage (physical strength), it is unjust to allow the other to perish. (Of course, if we apply Grotius' moral reasoning to this situation, it would not even be unjust to allow the other to perish. In fact, we are being perfectly just in saving our skin.) In the second story, willful deception is involved but once again because it is beneficial to the one committing injustice. A man tries to sell off burdensome or damaged assets (such as a house with serious defects or a rebellious slave) without revealing any of these defects to the buyer. The seller is being prudent in trying to get rid of what has become a burden to him. But he does so at the expense of someone else and even lies to that other party. (From the fair is foul, foul is fair perspective, it could of course be argued that nondisclosure is not the same as lying.)

To confuse things even more, the principles of justice and those of wisdom (*sapientia*) are presented as clashing with each other. According to Philus,

> Wisdom [*sapientia*] orders [us] to increase resources, to enlarge riches, to extend boundaries—for why was the praise carved on the monuments of the highest generals, "He advanced the boundaries of the empire," unless he had added something from another's [territory]?—to command as many persons as possible, to enjoy pleasures, to be powerful, to reign, to dominate. But justice instructs [us] to spare everyone, to take care of the human race, to render to each his own, not to touch sacred things, public things, another's things. Therefore, what is accomplished if you obey wisdom? Riches, powers, resources, honors, positions of command, kingdoms, for either private men or peoples.[8]

In the above fragment (of uncertain origin), wisdom is rendered equivalent to the self-interested thinking that legitimizes the pursuit of self-aggrandizement. This conception of "wisdom" is a prudential or utilitarian one, thereby conflicting with the Socratic (or Platonic) and religious understanding of wisdom.

The belief that passions that used to be condemned in fact have beneficial outcomes presupposes a focus on the external effects of self-interested actions. These external consequences are typically of a material (financial) nature. Socrates' approach, on the other hand, is what we could call pedagogical or psychological, in the broad sense of the term. He focusses on the consequences of injustice for the human soul (self). He invites his audience to look inward and to cease being fixated on outward appearances. Socrates eventually succeeds in getting others to agree with him that justice (*dikaiosuné*) refers to the "excellence and wisdom" of the soul.[9] He thereby corrects the materialistic "consequentialism" underlying the belief that injustice pays by connecting justice to personal "happiness" (*eudaimonia*) or blessedness. The latter does not consist in financial advantages or honors in the first place but in a unified soul, which is not something that is outwardly visible. Hence, a money-lover who is apparently just in his business transactions and "more outwardly decent than many" is able to repress other wrong desires, for instance, out of fear of losing his good reputation.[10] However, since money-making is his priority, "the true virtue of a balanced and well-adjusted soul would escape him by some long way."[11] In other words, as we have seen in the previous chapter, the just soul is a well-ordered soul who has got its priorities straight. This approach to justice, though certainly not adequate because of its rationalistic and individualistic premises, has the advantage of exposing the hypocrisy and incoherence of a "commercial" version of justice, in which the essential conflict between the love for justice and the love for money is deleted.

THE BOURGEOIS DELETION OF THE CONFLICT BETWEEN JUSTICE AND WEALTH

The ancient conviction that justice is to be preferred above utility and certainly above gain or profit clashes with a morality of self-interest. Note that I have not been saying that justice was always preferred to utility and profit in practice. That was certainly not the case. I am merely pointing out the premodern *consciousness* of a conflict between the passion for wealth and the quest for justice. Most of us will recognize the inner conflict and pain that we suffer when we must make choices that affect others negatively. Living with dilemmas is painful, and it is tedious to constantly try to find a way out. It is thus more tempting to negate the very existence of the dilemma between the self-interested pursuit of wealth and the full affirmation of the interests of others and to reject all thoughts that say otherwise as expressing "the romance of the old."[12] The passion for wealth obviously did not begin with capitalism or the modern age. Yet, there are two important differences between the premodern and modern passion for wealth. The first one is that the modern passion for wealth has lost its vile connotation. Our civilization has condoned materialism—made it a primary concern—and has even rebaptized greed as useful. As a result, the old conflict between justice and the passion for wealth has been erased or swept under the carpet. It is so much easier to pretend that foul is fair and that the desire for more benefits everyone. Insatiability, which used to be considered as a dangerous human inclination, has thus been released from its moral restraints. As the Skidelskys so aptly put it, we have made a pact with the Devil.[13] Such a pact, according to Keynes, is necessary, at least temporarily. The problem, of course, is that such a pact cannot be broken. Mephistopheles *possesses* Faust eternally. By turning societies into "economic societies" where the exchange and getting the best deal mentality prevails, we have similarly imprisoned ourselves in an endless materialistic spiral of means and ends. We try to escape the meaninglessness of our cage by attributing meanings to our material achievements. This is the second way in which the modern passion for wealth differs from the universal passion for comfort and wealth.

In *Economic Possibilities For Our Grandchildren*, Keynes voices his expectation that we shall someday be "free" and "return to some of the most sure and certain principles of religion and traditional virtue—that avarice is a vice, that the exaction of usury is a misdemeanor, and the love of money is detestable."[14] He thought that the return to the preference of virtue over the useful would happen naturally as people gradually satisfied their "economic necessities," and as a result, started to live in peace. In the meanwhile, we have to "pretend to ourselves and to everyone that fair is foul and foul is fair; for foul is useful and fair is not."[15] In other words, Keynes deplored the fact that traditional morality had to be sacrificed to fulfil "economic necessities," for the sake of a carefree and toilless future, but at the same time, he accepted this "fact" as dire necessity. Progress has its prices. Keynes was wrong for several reasons. One is the idea that the cause of war is economic "necessity," and correspondingly, that peace (and virtue) will follow from prosperity. He disregards the historical fact that wars are driven by the desire for power and superfluities and not so much for necessities. Another, related problem with his reasoning is that he overlooks the ways in which what he calls "economic necessities" have been created and are thus no "necessities" at all. In other words, Keynes ignores the blurring of the line between needs and wants and thus does not realize that these so-called necessities will continuously increase and will never be satisfied. Moreover, it is economically profitable to ensure that these necessities are multiplied.

The desire for more, however, is not simply the animal greed for goods. Wealth is not merely the means to consume or finance charities. Rousseau has convincingly argued that animal greed is not the dominant vice in modern, commercial societies. He understood that moderns are not greedy for objects but "greedy" for esteem. Wealth is not only the means to buy things but also and specially to acquire status. A higher salary, a more expensive car, or house, designer clothing and shoes, and accessories such as exclusive watches, jewelry, and bags are markers of higher status. As Rousseau writes:

> One does everything to become rich but only to be esteemed. This is proven by the fact that instead of limiting oneself to the mediocrity that constitutes well-being, everyone wants to reach a degree of wealth that attracts attention but also leads to increased cares and troubles and becomes nearly as burdensome as poverty itself. This is again proven by the ridiculous use that the wealthy make of their wealth.[16]

Rousseau sees the struggle for recognition (i.e., to be recognized as superior to others) as one of the most powerful drives in modern life. As I observed in the previous chapter, this drive is more widespread in societies where individuals constantly compare themselves with each other and derive their self-worth through this comparison. In the context of economism and financialism, such worth depends on productivity and pecuniary wealth. We try to gain such recognition especially through our wealth, consumption patterns, and work (career). The "bandwagon, snob and Veblen effects" illustrate the insight that goods are not desired merely for their utility. Goods are desired because others have them (bandwagon); because others do not have them (snob) and because they are reputed to be expensive (Veblen).[17] People are willing to pay for "exclusivity." This desire to distinguish ourselves from others, to impress and surpass others in outward appearance is a natural aspect and consequence of a culture in which civic friendship and justice (in the sense explained at the outset) are secondary concerns.

The aspiration to climb the social ladder is often tied up with bourgeois morality. This association is confirmed by McCloskey in several of her works, even though she calls that drive "innovation."[18] As I observed earlier, McCloskey appears to consider bourgeois morality as a universal morality that we all *ought* to embrace. She and Carden thus speak of the "Bourgeois Era."[19] Though we are at liberty to disagree with her normative claim, she is not completely wrong to refer to our age as the Bourgeois Era. Of course, if we accept this premise, we must agree that the most systematized forms of dehumanization (through the "satanic mills," for instance) and efficient forms of mass murder have also been devised in that same era. That cannot only be an unfortunate coincidence or the result of "antibourgeois nostalgias."[20] Innovation is certainly a double-edged sword. For the present purpose, let me restrict my focus to the universalization of the bourgeois mentality, which has resulted in the dissolution of the conflict between utility, gain, and wealth, on the one hand, and justice, on the other. I think that Mumford fittingly captures this cultural shift. As he writes,

> With the weakening of caste lines and the development of bourgeois individualism the ritual of conspicuous expenditure spread rapidly throughout the rest of society: it justified the abstractions of the money-makers and put to wider uses the technical progress of the inventors. The ideal of a powerful expensive life supplanted the ideal of a holy or a humane one. Heaven, which had been deferred to the Hereafter in the scheme of the Christian cosmos, was now to be enjoyed immediately: its streets paved the precious stones, its glittering walls, its marbled halls, were almost at hand—provided one had acquired money enough to buy them.[21]

This type of materialism is no longer restricted to one particular "class." It has been universalized through the democratization of societies. Everyone is brought up with the belief that she can and should climb the social ladder to be somebody.

This belief or expectation, which is aroused by formal equality, clashes with factual socioeconomic inequalities. The discrepancy between the narrative of equality and the factual impossibility of such equality leads to *ressentiment*.[22] This discrepancy is strangely enough overlooked by the proponents of capitalism and laissez-faireism. One such tireless advocate is McCloskey. Though a self-professed liberal and an apparent defender of human freedom, that liberalism of hers is tainted with contempt for all that is not bourgeois. She would deny that bourgeois aspirations reflect the desire to live the aristocratic life, as Molière has satirized in *Le Bourgeois gentilhomme* (1670). She would disagree with the observation that there is a conflict between gain and justice since the clever entrepreneur has the right to a reward for his courage. In fact, bourgeois life provides us with innumerable opportunities to become virtuous. Of all virtues, prudence is perhaps *the* bourgeois virtue par excellence, or so McCloskey says. She and Carden define it as follows:

> It's the virtue of buying low and selling high. It's the virtue that causes you to ask whether you *really* need to buy another pair of shoes when you already have so many given that the money could be used elsewhere. It's the virtue that causes you to sell your car when you live in downtown Chicago and it's clear that you're probably better served just taking taxis and Uber and Lyft everywhere. It is the virtue that knows when to stop instead of continuing to press forward with work, work, *work* that, thanks to the law of diminishing marginal returns, isn't adding as much as you might think. A business-loving civilization is one soaked with applied prudence.[23]

Bourgeois civilization described this way seems so idyllic, uncomplicated and nearly innocent. The complexity of the real world is left out, and the contractual model of human relations is sanctioned.

Asymmetrical power relations and the not-so-innocent passions and practices that determine the rules of the game are conveniently overlooked. Instead, we are made to believe that it is a fair game in which all actors have equal chances. We do not get to read anything about the miserable plight of the people from whom the businessperson "buys low" and of those who cannot afford the basic necessities of life because the businessperson "sells high." The struggle for existence of many forced to participate in the gig economy is ignored. The decision to work or to stop working is presented as an individual choice. The fact that wealth is often accumulated to the detriment of others does not fit in the idyllic picture of the "business-loving civilization." Quite unsurprisingly, McCloskey claims that rich (countries) became rich through their creativity, enabled by capitalism. Her rose-colored glasses conveniently leave out the role of imperialism and colonialism, as well as slave trade and of enclosure in generating prosperity. We should feel guilty about human evils but not about the riches since those evils did not lead to riches—or so she claims. McCloskey does not tolerate divergent views on these issues, including various interpretations of human history and of its driving forces. Her apology for American capitalism is the old and wearisome narrative of progress:

> If we have our wits about us we can in the next fifty years use up the oil in the Middle East and yet replace it in automobiles and heating with hydrogen. We can drain the Oglala aquifer in the next twenty years, and yet one day replenish it—mad thought—from desalinized seawater piped to Nebraska using that cheap and clean hydrogen fuel, if we have our wits about us. The modern world is different from a zero-sum world, which Malthus theorized just as it was disappearing forever. We can keep on innovating, keep up the factor of 8.5 or 19.[24]

In her Max Weber lecture entitled "Bourgeois Towns: How Capitalism Became Virtuous 1600–1776," delivered on December 19, 2007 at the European University Institute, McCloskey notes that "all of them, Hume, Rousseau, Smith, Hegel, Tönnies, Durkheim, and even, a late instance, on many points Max Weber, and still later Karl Polanyi got the historical facts quite wrong."[25]

The crux of the matter, however, is not merely about getting the "facts" right. Instead, intellectual probity demands that we ask ourselves whether we academics are not legitimizing injustice through our narratives. It is comfortable to deny the fact that prosperity has its prices and that the prevailing form of economic life is unjust (and thrives on injustice). Such denial helps us to ease our consciences and exempts us from the uncomfortable task of reconciling utility with justice. It "liberates" us from accepting and carrying the responsibility for our fellow beings. The separative model of the human informs McCloskey's thought but also that of Keynes. We may wonder whether the latter really believed in a future in which traditional morality would be restored. As it happens, he does not seem to have had much faith in human nature. The money-making game, he notes in his *General Theory*, should not be banned since it canalizes "dangerous human proclivities."[26] He thought that such commitment to wealth accumulation would distract people from "cruelty, the reckless pursuit of personal power and authority, and other forms of self-aggrandisement."[27] Human reality, however, is messier: the passion for wealth usually goes hand in hand with the will-to-power, cruelty, and the desire for self-aggrandizement. More relevantly here, the strong utilitarian tendency of the fair is foul, foul is fair reasoning should be highlighted. Keynes implies that we can and should be willing to live as bandits and, even more so, as bandits who live individual lives without fellowship with each other—since human fellowship is not possible if we believe that foul is fair, and fair is foul.

THE GOODNESS OF LIMITS

Students of economics learn about the distinction between needs and wants, and they usually get acquainted with Abraham Maslow's hierarchy of needs.[28] They may also believe that the raison d'être of the economy is to fulfil these needs. In this sense, they may truly think that they are contributing to human flourishing since the fulfilment of basic necessities is a precondition for such flourishing.[29] However, they will most probably quickly forget these fundamental distinctions as they learn to think in terms of preferences, models, games, and utility maximization. The language of needs will become incoherent as they come to realize that economies thrive on wants. As I admitted earlier, the re-introduction of the idea of "needs" raises difficulties, and some of these are unsurmountable, at least within the scope of the present work. What we consider to be "needs" are dangerous superfluities for others. This is illustrated by the dialogue between Socrates and Glaucon in Plato's *Politeia*. What Socrates considers to be an ideal, balanced city-state is condemned by Glaucon as being a "city of pigs."[30] What Glaucon considers to be normal is for Socrates a luxurious state "filled with hordes of people who are no longer in our states for essential purposes."[31] These include more doctors due to the decadent way of eating and living in such a state. The idea that immoderate desires are the sources of moral and physical disorders is one that I believe must be recalled if we wish to check and correct the dehumanizing effects of the reversal of traditional morality.

I do not claim that there is an objective and universal measure of genuine needs, especially since the latter are not solely material. Yet, if we do wish to address our politico-economic and ecological predicaments, we must cultivate an awareness of a demarcation between "needs" and "wants," between absolute needs and relative needs, between genuine and false needs, even if no fixed line can be drawn between them. It is an imperative that we regain the notion of limits, not only because this is just but also for the sake of our own well-being. As Mumford so unequivocally observes:

> Vital wants are all necessarily limited. Just as the organism itself does not continue to grow beyond the norm of its species, a norm established within relatively narrow limits, so neither can any particular function of life be satisfied by limitless indulgence. [. . .] Healthy activity requires restriction, monotony, repetition, as well as change, variety, and expansion. The querulous boredom of a child that possesses too many toys is endlessly repeated in the lives of the rich who, having no pecuniary limit to the expression of their desires, are unable without tremendous force of character to restrict themselves to a single channel long enough to profit by its trenching and deepening and wearing through.[32]

Unlimited and disordered desires follow from the absence of the notion of limited needs, which is the recipe for fragmented personhoods. Isn't it strange that most of us do have a notion of needs and limits when we bring up our children but "forget" it in the world of adults?

Another reason for drawing a line between genuine and false needs is in order to prevent us from forgetting and neglecting our real needs. Not only unlimited wants but also unfulfilled and unrecognized needs are the causes of disorders because their unfulfillment fragilizes our selves. Moreover, we may unwittingly try to fulfil them in inappropriate, violent, or self-destructive ways. The absolute or basic needs of the human are both material and spiritual (in the sense of pertaining to the human spirit). This is well-illustrated by Weil's conceived set of needs. According to her, the needs of the human soul are the need for order, liberty, obedience, responsibility, equality, hierarchy, honor, punishment, freedom of expression, security, risk, private property, collective property, and truth, "more sacred than any other."[33] Similarly, for Mumford, vital human needs are more than animal needs:

> Song, story, music, painting, carving, idle play, drama—all these things lie outside the province of animal necessities; but they are not things which are to be included after the belly is satisfied; they are functions which must be included in human existence even to satisfy the belly, to say nothing of the emotional and intellectual and imaginative needs of man.[34]

The Skidelskys' more recent list of "basic goods" comprises health, security, respect, personality (and because of the latter, private property), harmony with nature, friendship (*philia*), and leisure.[35] These needs are often in conflict with each other: order versus liberty, obedience versus responsibility, equality versus hierarchy, private versus collective property, and so on. The fulfilment of these needs therefore requires their reconciliation in such a way that a just equilibrium is reached and none of these needs is neglected or ignored.

Such an equilibrium has been lost. Even worse, there is no attempt to reach one because the very idea of an equilibrium is absent. Practically, we (unconsciously) try to reconcile conflicting commitments since we cannot possibly be in two places at the same time. Yet, we do not necessarily give up certain desires, even if they happen to contradict each other; and we do not necessarily rank them. Concretely, it means that we would like to be in these two places at the same time. This is one of the reasons why we are glued to our phones and screens, even during conversations, meetings, lectures, and meals. As a result, our attention is fragmented. Some of us consider it normal to devote more time and attention to gaming and watching sports than to caring, group or collaborative activities. Historians of economic thought and even economists tend to blame fellow economists and certain schools of economic thought for the levelling down of qualitative distinctions between different desires. The Skidelskys thus observe:

> The various distinctions drawn by pre-modern economic thought—between needs and wants, necessities and luxuries, use—and exchange- value—all rest on the assumption that some ways of life are intrinsically superior to others. Modern economics has dispensed with this assumption.[36]

I am slightly more reluctant to consider economists and economics as the main culprits. The claims of economists admittedly do have far-reaching consequences, especially at the policy level. However, as it should appear from the above examples, the levelling down of distinctions is a cultural phenomenon. Economics as a discipline tends to assimilate cultural shifts and trends in other disciplines and thus rarely originates new paradigms. This assimilation capacity also explains the pluralism within the discipline itself.

The levelling down of qualitative distinctions between desires could be conceived as a corruption or side-effect of "democratization." Plato would disagree that it is a corruption or side-effect since he believed that all desires are equal for the democrat as such. His view of the democrat—and hence not of the corrupted democrat, as I am suggesting—is not very flattering:

> He [the democrat] won't accept a true account nor admit it to his stronghold if anyone tells him that some pleasures belong to good, worthwhile desires, others to bad ones, and that he must practice and respect the former, and hold the latter in check and control them. But he denies all of this and says they

> are all alike and must be treated as equals. [. . .] Therefore he lives and enjoys the desire that each day happens to bring along, sometimes indulging in wine to the sound of the flute, and at others drinking water and pining away. Again there are times when he takes exercise, but there are times when he's idle and neglects everything, while at others he's apparently engrossed in philosophy [. . .]; and there is no order or necessity in his life, but he calls this existence truly pleasant and free and blessed and applies himself to it throughout the whole of his life.[37]

Plato is portraying the person with an unordered soul. We do not have to believe that those who are committed to equality and freedom are necessarily such disordered souls. However, in chapter two, I referred to Buber's insightful observation that the abstract ideals of equality and freedom must be held together by a lived fraternity. Only then do we have genuine equality and genuine freedom. Otherwise, these ideals turn into the desire to possess and for power.[38] The above fragment does illustrate what it means to live without distinction between various desires, and such levelling down, as I have been arguing, is a feature of our culture.

What does the negation of distinction and order have got to do with "democratization?" As I noted earlier, we are here dealing with a cultural phenomenon. It is related to "democratization" insofar as the latter has gone hand in hand with the negation of hierarchies. The passion for equality does not necessarily lead to a levelling down of values, but when this passion is accompanied by a revolt against all that which reminds us of the older way of life, we may throw the baby out with the bathwater. That said, the story is much more complex and involves much more than democratization and its side effects. "Democratization" itself is likely to be conceived in different ways. Scholars tend to disagree on the question regarding its early beginnings and its motives or causes. The various factors that could possibly have contributed to the levelling down of qualitative distinctions between desires—at the cultural level—are too innumerable to be mentioned in a few sentences. Moreover, such a historical exercise falls beyond the scope of the present book. What I do want to highlight is that we have inherited certain ideas, beliefs, and ways of doing things that have a long history. The foul is fair, fair is foul perspective did not come up because a few men devised it. We have got used to the notion that we should get what we want. The notion that what we want—even if it harmless and blameless—may not be in accordance with our vocation and a higher norm of justice will sound nonsensical (and antiquated). Consider, for instance, typical birthday wishes such as "may your wishes or dreams come true" or "may you get what you want." The idea that our wishes and dreams may not be the right ones is conspicuously absent. These habits of the heart and mind cannot be changed at the push of a button.

Therefore, it is not superfluous to remind ourselves that we have acquired these habits and that they are not necessarily good.

I must perhaps add that certain aspirations are not absolutely higher than others but are better relatively to the way of life that befits each one of us. Consider once again Weil's set of needs above. Though freedom of expression is an absolute human need, it can be surmised that it is a greater need for the writer and journalist than for the toddler. Similarly, private property will have less value for a person who has chosen to live in a commune than for a family. Of course, even that person will need a minimum of private space and have some personal belongings. If the writer and journalist misuse their freedom of expression for money, status, or any other advantage, they would then be neglecting a need that is proper to their vocation. Their hierarchy of desires (needs) would then be corrupted. Correspondingly, they would then be untrue to themselves and their vocation. Certain desires (needs) become stronger or weaker as we grow older. Our interests or commitments change. The desire to carry responsibility, for example, usually grows as we get older. As a result, we devote less time to play and more time to study, care, work, and community and civic service. It is noteworthy that Weil conceived responsibility as a human need. It is a "need" because the capacity for responsibility—that is, to respond to the demands that arise by virtue of our place in the world—is one of the defining features of the human person. Heschel thus writes that a human being "would cease to be a self if he were to be deprived of responsibility."[39] Similarly, the person who refuses to carry the responsibilities incumbent on her refuses to be a human self. In the previous chapter, I have noted that the desire to be a human self must be awakened and kept alive and that we need others to help us do so. More generally speaking, certain passions can restrain other, lower passions and prevent them from dominating the whole soul. For example, the love for justice can curb our passion for comfort.

Genuine self-fulfillment thus requires limits and order. Accordingly, an "Economics of Enough" is not only necessary because of the depletion of resources but is also inherently good.[40] It is in accordance with a truer understanding of the human. Though lack of moderation leads to conflicts over "scarce resources," moderation in itself is a good because excesses undermine our very humanity and prevent us from becoming wholesome selves. More positively formulated, simplicity and sobriety are conducive to genuine human flourishing. The person who accepts limits is "happier," Augustine notes:

> Of these two men, let us suppose that one is poor, or, better, in moderate circumstance; the other, extremely wealthy. But, our wealthy man is haunted by fear, heavy with cares, feverish with greed, never secure, always restless,

> breathless from endless quarrels with his enemies. By these miseries, he adds to his possessions beyond measure, but he also piles up for himself a mountain of distressing worries. That man of modest means is content with a small and compact patrimony. He is loved by his own, enjoys the sweetness of peace in his relations with kindred, neighbors, and friends, is religious and pious, of kindly disposition, healthy in body, self-restrained, chaste in morals, and at peace with his conscience. I wonder if there is anyone so senseless as to hesitate over which of the two to prefer. What is true of these two individuals is likewise true of two families, two nations, two kingdoms; the analogy holds in both cases.[41]

The distinction between needs and wants, the necessary and the superflous, is an essential feature of premodern thought, ancient and early modern forms of republicanism, and nonmainstream understandings of development. It is therefore an important aspect of Rousseau's thought, which I now briefly examine. He shows how unlimited needs disintegrate both selves and societies.

Rousseau distinguishes between absolute needs and less absolute needs.[42] We have physical needs that pertain to our physical survival (food, sleep, clothing, and shelter in colder climates). A second set of needs includes sex and all other things that promote our comfort and general well-being. These desires, according to him, can be resisted without leading to death.[43] There is a third set of needs peculiar to us humans due to our moral (or spiritual) nature.[44] The needs for friendship, honor, and recognition belong to the third category. Such moral needs are largely dependent on imagination and public opinion. Their expansion, according to Rousseau, can cause more havoc than voluptuous desires and ordinary greed (for more food and clothes, for instance). In fact, what appears to be simple greed is often fueled by the desire for status or prestige (which belongs to the spiritual type of need). Happiness, for him, therefore consists in curbing our imagination and re-evaluating public opinion. The free human being is not a slave of ever-increasing desires but is instead characterized by the balance between her needs and her power to fulfil these.[45] Though it is historically true that our "needs" have increased as our power has increased (especially through technology), it does not mean that the balance can constantly be regained. Desires typically increase disproportionally, largely due to an unbridled imagination. Hence, though Rousseau warns against the "underutilization" of our faculties, he does not advocate an indiscriminate enhancement of our power.[46] Unlimited development leads to the degeneration of society because all are wholeheartedly preoccupied with self-aggrandizement. In such a state, the notion of a common good that transcends clashing individual interests is lost. A corruption of mores, weak governments, and the disintegration of the political community ensue.[47]

In advocating an Economics of Enough, I am not glorifying primitivism and poverty, especially the forms of poverty that have arisen through industrialization, colonialization, wars, and climate change. There are forms of destitution that dehumanize and lead to depravity, but these, paradoxically enough, are often the results of a particular caste's unrestrained passion for wealth, political imprudence, and despotism. Obviously, the notion of needs and limits is a prerequisite for just international relations. Once the richer countries acknowledge the fact that they have disregarded the needs of others and have been living off their backs, they might be willing to bear the greater burdens of the crises inherent to the Anthropocene. The political disregard of needs and limits has led to the destruction of the habitat of countless beings, satanic mills (that are still existent), dehumanization, the polarization of societies between poor and rich, between rural and urban, and a precarious future for those after us. Producing, consuming, and living as if tomorrow will care for itself is the antithesis of what Schumacher calls an "economics of permanence."[48] It is the antithesis of wisdom, freedom, and peace. As he notes,

> Every increase of needs tends to increase one's dependence on outside forces over which one cannot have control, and therefore increases existential fear. Only by a reduction of needs can one promote a genuine reduction in those tensions which are the ultimate causes of strife and war.[49]

Schumacher proves Keynes wrong. Too many wants, and not necessities, are the primary source of discord and war.

THE ILLUSION OF FAIR MARKETS

In the introduction, I argued that a wholesome economy depends on good governance. Such good governance will be based on some notion of the needs of a people, the needs of other peoples, and hence of limits. National economies in today's world are admittedly not solely governed by national governments because other global actors also influence the direction and substance of economies. However, the government of a democratic people has the responsibility to protect the latter from dehumanizing forces. It can still choose to promote and discourage certain economic activities, production and consumption through its regulations and investments. It can choose to protect certain sectors of the national economy from the forces of international markets. In other words, it can determine the extent to which it wants the national economy to be subjected to the rules of international forces. Am I here advocating "socialism," "communism," or "protectionism"? Not exactly. I am instead recalling the basic tenets of democratic life. Accordingly, I wish to dispel the illusion that free markets are the most efficient, serve the interests of all, and are fair. Such an illusion rests on other illusions, flawed ideas, and an alienating conception of human nature. One such misconception is the myth of a harmony of interests, whereby individual interests and the general interest are conceived in material terms (self-enrichment and GDP). Once material welfare had become an overriding concern in early modern times, the neutralization of vices followed quite naturally. The creation of "free markets" manifests the political endorsement of the latter flawed idea, at the expense of civic friendship and justice. It is no news that free markets "protect" the individual freedom of entrepreneurs. But this freedom, as I observed above, becomes the will to profit and to power if it is not embedded in fraternal relationships.

The economy, like all human affairs, must be governed to universal ends. Political nonaction, which also includes little structural control of economic actors, means giving free rein to private or corporate powers to determine the fate of whole societies. The tendency to defensively label all attempts to transcend laissez-faire ideology as socialism or communism reflects the tenacity of the belief in free markets. It is significant that Paul Krugman, in his introduction to the new edition of Keynes' *General Theory*, emphasizes that "Keynes was no socialist—he came to save capitalism, not to bury it."[50] Krugman, however, does add that "free-market fundamentalists are right to hate Keynes" since the latter did not believe that markets left to themselves without any government intervention at all would produce "the best of all possible worlds."[51] Coyle correctly notes that the "'states versus markets' perspective is bogus. Debates about the scope of government intervention on close inspection turn out to be about the nature of government intervention."[52] Markets function in a given context, which may be one of a strong nation-state or an absent nation-state where the rule of law is absent; a strong democracy or, on the contrary, a corrupt, weak democracy where civic friendship and justice are absent. Similarly, Strange notes that "it is very easily forgotten that markets exist under the authority and by permission of the state, and are conducted on whatever terms the state may choose to dictate, or allow."[53] In this sense, markets are not "value free." On the contrary, as Coyle remarks, "actual markets in actual economies embody the social norms and underlying values of the societies in which they operate [. . .] Markets need an effective state to operate well, and a healthy state will in turn depend on a thriving market sector of the economy."[54]

Both Coyle and Strange presume "embedded" markets, that is, markets that are imbued with the values that constitute the societies of which they are part. That might have been the case if the idea of a market economy and, even worse, of a "market society" had not been born. That very idea reflects the separative understanding of human nature and the view of society as an aggregation of atoms. The two economists justly recall that economic actors do not operate in a vacuum but in a sociopolitical context. Moreover, their emphasis on the human dimension of markets is correct and needed. Markets are no neutral exchange mechanisms. "Immoral" or unjust markets reflect human wickedness and thoughtlessness both at the personal and cultural levels. Market failures, therefore, cannot only be blamed on information asymmetry. Yet, Coyle's argument that the market is socially embedded does not hold water in our present context. She overlooks the essential differences between the premodern and modern cultural contexts, including the novel notion that vices (such as vanity and money-making) are not so bad after all. Globalization, that is, the globalization of the idea of a market economy only helps to spread the plague of individualistic irresponsibility. Polanyi explains that markets in the premodern context were meeting places that functioned without the economy. As he writes:

> Markets through which otherwise self-sufficient householders get rid of their surplus neither direct production nor provide the producer with his income. This is only the case in a market-economy where *all* incomes derive from sales, and commodities are obtainable exclusively by purchase.[55]

The ambition to create a "market economy," unique in history, results in the disembedding of the economy—and certainly of the market—from societal control and norms (such as obligations and reciprocity). Polanyi thus notes that "to allow the market mechanism to be sole director of the fate of human beings and their natural environment indeed [. . .] would result in the demolition of society."[56] This is why a "market society" is a contradiction in terms.

A "market economy" has been a failed experiment; a true "market economy" does not exist. As Coyle points out, we should not confuse "the economy" with "the market" even if these two terms tend to be used indistinguishably. Contemporary economies include "households and families, businesses, not-for-profits, unions, and indeed different bodies and branches of the state."[57] In other words, part of the real economy takes place outside the market and often does not involve exchange and money. Proponents of more laissez-faireism long for a condition that comes close to that ideal situation (a "market economy") where they would be "free" to explore all opportunities and "buy low and sell high."[58] It is perhaps not so surprising that the socioeconomically successful propound a romantic image of the market as a fair exchange place for peace-loving, trusting, and trustworthy actors. This image is reinforced by a few interpersonal transactions that appear to be fair.[59] However, the more profound observers and the many struggling people in the real world confirm the image of the market, as we know it today, as a jungle where the powerful survive. As Bourdieu writes:

> Dominant firms exert their pressure on the dominated firms and on their strategies: they define the *regularities* and sometimes the *rules* of the game, by imposing the definition of strengths most favourable to their interests and modifying the entire environment of the other firms and the system of constraints that bear on them or the space of possibles offered to them.[60]

Actual markets today are not organic parts of particular societies because they are international markets. They are certainly governed by certain rules and they certainly reflect certain values. The latter, however, are those of the most powerful players, who also set the rules of the game. When weaker national economies participate in these international markets, they must comply with the rules set by others and accept the values of the powerful. This is the extent to which markets are "fair."

Given these asymmetrical power relations and unlimited wants, it should be clear that market prices do not indicate how much must be produced and are thus not self-evidently the best way of allocating resources to fulfil the needs of a people. I am thereby not saying that "a small committee can have godlike knowledge of the whole economic order."[61] This tendency to think in terms of polarities, namely, "market" and "centralized economic planning" is not very helpful but, even more importantly, reflects the absence of the notion of a people or democratic community and local democratic communities. The image of the government as an overseer and of the rest as a collection of individuals informs the thinking of many market advocates. This image, rather than the actual untrustworthiness of governments (as well as their alienation from a large percentage of the people), seems to motivate the nearly principled distrust of government. I will come back to this phenomenon. For the time being, let us consider the oft-voiced argument that market prices are the most reliable guides for producers, consumers, and other parties (such as governments and investors). Coyle thus notes that only "markets can convey the vast array of detailed information about preferences, incomes, the demands of buyers, and the costs of sellers."[62] This reasoning *might* have been valid in a world of equal and fair players but is clearly flawed in a world of unequal power. Prices in the real world are determined by those who have a greater market share and those who conspire to fix prices that are most advantageous to them.[63] Coyle is aware of the serious limitations and failures of the market. She thus correctly notes that market prices do not take externalities such as pollution and other harmful effects into account.[64] Yet, there is much more that is not reflected in prices.

More fundamentally, market prices do not reflect the real costs of production, which include real labor costs (which must be wages sufficient to live a human life), the depletion of natural "resources," the genuine costs of product destruction, environmental and social impacts that will only be visible in the future, and the social and health impacts of the consumption of certain products. By now, we all know that the costs of producers of, for example, coffee, tea, and cacao are not covered by the *market* prices that they get for their produce. The low incomes that farmers receive have resulted in destitution, child labor, and deforestation. The inhumane conditions on tea plantations (starvation wages, slavery, and ill-treatment) have been exposed by journalists and anti-slavery and human rights watch organizations.[65] The buyer (trader) is here the one who determines the price. The farmer can take it or leave it. Similarly, high prices of basic necessities such as grains do not necessarily reflect shortages. Grain traders (buyers) are powerful enough to manipulate prices and to buy so low that producers receive incomes that are below subsistence levels.[66] Anti-monopoly laws might be able to reduce the unhealthy concentrations of power in the hands of a few traders in global food supply chains.[67] However, the right to food would necessitate government intervention to ensure that food remains affordable for all and that those at the bottom of the food supply chain receive a fair income. The food sovereignty movement is a powerful response to the broken food system.

The market fails at a fundamental level because, as Schumacher notes, it does not distinguish between primary and secondary goods and thereby ignores the incommensurability of various categories of goods.[68] It belongs to the essence of the market that everything should be equated with everything else. This means that primary goods, derived from nature (such as oil, coal, and agricultural produce), are treated in the same way as secondary goods (manufactured products). The effacement of the qualitative distinction between the primary good on which the secondary product is dependent—combined with the higher status of man-made things—has led to the downgrading of the primary. Schumacher therefore rightly points out that the metaphysical question of whether agriculture is essentially different from industry is rarely raised. The difference, he notes, is one "between life and death":

> The fundamental "principle" of agriculture is that it deals with life, that is to say, with living substances. Its products are the results of processes of life and its means of production is the living soil [. . .] "Agricultural operations" involve more than the production of incomes and the lowering of costs. What is involved is the whole relationship between man and nature, the whole life-style of a society, the health, happiness and harmony of man, as well as the beauty of his habitat.[69]

A precarious primary sector, where small farmers are constantly struggling to survive, is a consequence of the monetization of all primary goods and of their relatively low pricing.

This low pricing can be explained by the higher prestige attached to being a homo faber as opposed to being an animal laborans, to borrow Arendt's terminology. Accordingly, the "work of our hands" is valued more highly than the "labor of our bodies."[70] Similarly, Mumford writes:

> The symbol of price made direct seizure and gratification vulgar: so that finally the farmer who produced enough fruit and meat and vegetables to satisfy his hunger felt a little inferior to the man who, producing these goods for the market, could buy back the inferior products of the packing house and the cannery. [. . .] Money became the symbol of reputable consumption in every aspect of living, from art and education to marriage and religion.[71]

While the animal laborans understands himself as part of nature, the homo faber sees himself as "lord and master of the whole earth."[72] The basic attitude of the homo faber is thus the instrumental mentality: all things are degraded into means or commodities, which means that they are emptied of their—or, denied any—intrinsic value.[73] This is exactly what has happened to labor and land, which are obviously no commodities.[74] The failure to realize that nature is not necessarily up for grabs leads to the privatization of the "commons," the trampling of tribal rights, including their rights to sacred ground, destruction of farming grounds, earthquakes, and water pollution (thereby affecting marine life).[75] The mining of certain minerals—used in mobile phones, computers, and jewelry—has gone hand in hand with conditions of slavery, (sexual) abuses, murders, and a general state of corruption.[76]

Actual markets in the actual world are anything but fair. They are not best left "free" to guarantee the best outcomes. That freedom, I have been arguing, gives the powerful free rein to oppress the weaker because markets are no neutral space where equal players meet. Whoever wants to join the game must comply with the rules that have been devised by the dominant parties. Whoever wants to play must also accept the values supporting the market. These values, however, are not those that constitute a society. The market, instead, "is the institutionalization of individualism and non-responsibility [since] neither buyer nor seller is responsible for anything but himself."[77] It could be replied that such individualism and ethos of nonresponsibility are characteristic of the prevailing culture (and not so much of the "market"). The chronic housing shortage and soaring prices of houses that have been affecting so many people around the world would arguably be less severe if some of us, including the political representatives of a people, did not deem it "necessary" to possess several houses, large estates, and mansions. The fact that such greed is not condemned and not checked in a *democracy* illustrates the undemocratic nature of our prevailing culture. Modern markets do seem to reinforce the sense of nonresponsibility and selfishness. Markets are not actual, physical marketplaces where fellow beings meet and fulfil transactions. They are virtual and impersonal, and left to themselves or, rather to the anonymous players that dominate them, they do not guarantee justice. Moreover, we must not forget the main motive behind the aspiration to a market economy, namely, the love of profit. There is an essential conflict between the market mentality, on the one hand, and civic friendship and justice, on the other.

RE-EMBEDDING THE MARKET

A socially embedded market would be one that is directed toward fulfilling truly universal ends. The legal and normative framework within which it functions would reflect universal values, that is, those values that foster a life proper to humans and maintain a wholesome relation between humans and their natural environment. This means that though markets—being human institutions—are always driven and supported by particular values, the latter need not be humane and humanizing values. Moreover, the original motives behind a "market society" should not be forgotten even if we no longer identify with them. The desire to break from the social bonds that hampered "innovation" and profit is one of them. The loss of the sense of being part of a social body also played an important role, despite not being a motive as such. It is part of the new self-understanding that sustains the new form of individualism. The dissolution of the social body was already taking place in the seventeenth century as society increasingly came to be conceived as a collection of individuals who interact through economic exchange.[78] It is quite likely that it was not only an idea but also the actual experience of people. Ontology and phenomenology are intimated connected.[79] The utopian and nearly "religious" character of the aspiration for a market society must also be highlighted. The belief that a self-regulating market system could control a whole economy (and thus society) and automatically solve the problems that arise is impressive. It is significant that Mary L. Hirschfeld claims that "the real power of economics lies [. . .] in its reassuring insight that markets can channel self-interested or even outright selfish behavior into socially desirable outcomes."[80] A strange unwillingness to carry the burden of human responsibility for human affairs seems to be latently present in this faith.

The re-embeddedness of the market would thus require the transcendence of all forms of determinism—as Strange has convincingly and relentlessly argued—and the acknowledgment of the political responsibility and power to direct markets to universal human ends. Things are much more complicated in the case of international markets, as I have observed above. Particular governments may be committed to human values and may wish to protect their peoples from ruthless so-called economic laws. However, their room for maneuver may not be very big if their economies are dependent on international markets and if they themselves are not the powerful players. Policies and regulations seem to have been serving the interests of the powerful.[81] As Strange observed:

> The dominant trend in United States domestic policy-making through the past decade [since the 1970s] under Presidents Ford and Carter, as well as President Reagan, has been toward deregulation. [. . .] Cloaked (as policy often is) in the fine-sounding rhetoric of liberal ideology, it was actually driven in the latter case by the very strong material interests of some of the biggest and most successful American corporations and their banks, supported by their lobbyists in Washington and promulgated by influential writers, journals and newspapers.[82]

The unhealthy power of financial and corporate lobbyists has been frequently mentioned in academic literature, investigative articles, and popular media. It is remarkable that this power is still unchanged.

Governments seem unwilling to take the measures that are necessary to liberate the real economy from the grips and fickleness of the financial sector. This has led many to identify the recurrent financial and hence economic crises as a failure of politics.[83] Only government intervention can address the instability of the international financial system and reduce the great disparities in wealth since it was political decision that released the monster in the first place. Keynes is therefore right in pointing to the wisdom behind old usury laws. Many today probably share his hope for the "euthanasia of the rentier."[84] Bernie Sanders' proposition to close Wall Street was not as ludicrous at it might have seemed.[85] Strange thought that the permanent closure of the City (closed during the war) would "have been better than the consequences of Harold Wilson's first unthinking (and typically shortsighted) steps to hasten its rebirth."[86] Keynes, similarly, suggested measures to mitigate the influence of the speculators of Wall Street and the City on the course of investments. "Casinos," he notes, "should, in the public interest, be inaccessible and expensive."[87] Since stock exchanges follow the logic of gambling, the "introduction of a substantial government transfer tax on all transactions" would help to reduce their frequency and the stakes of the game.[88] The Skidelskys also suggest taxing "trades in financial instruments like derivatives."[89] This, according to them, would reduce the power of the financial sector and finance useful public spending. These are a few examples of the unpopular measures that could be taken to re-create the legal and moral framework within which markets function. Agriculture would require an altogether different approach and system of pricing, including more local markets. Clearly, the transition to a life-centered economy requires that we articulate the higher ends that are served by these unpopular measures. Only then can we re-establish the norms and limits that are absolutely indispensable for a human life.

NOTES

1. Plato, *Republic, Volume I*, 49 (Book I).
2. Ibid, 69–71 (Book I).
3. Ibid, 123, 131, 153 (Book II).
4. Ibid, 71 (Book I).
5. The problem with these particular fragments is that they are not necessarily literal citations but instead interpretations that reflect the Christian ideal of universal justice. Moreover, the writings of pre-Christian philosophers are used to support Christian apologetics, both positively and negatively. In the latter case, a caricatural portrayal of "pagan" practices is not uncommon.
6. Cicero, *On the Republic*, 93 (Book III).
7. Ibid, 95–96.
8. Ibid, 97.
9. Plato, *Republic, Volume I*, 101 (Book I).
10. Plato, *Republic, Volume II*, 247 (Book VIII).
11. Ibid.
12. Cf. McCloskey, *The Bourgeois Virtues*, 31.
13. Skidelsky and Skidelsky, *How Much is Enough?*, 7.
14. Keynes, "Economic Possibilities for Our Grandchildren (1930)," 330–331.
15. Ibid, 331.
16. Jean-Jacques Rousseau, "Fragments politiques," in *Œuvres complètes de Jean-Jacques Rousseau III*, eds. Bernard Gagnebin and Marcel Raymond (Paris: Editions Gallimard, 1964), 502.
17. Skidelsky and Skidelsky, *How Much is Enough?*, 38.
18. Carden and McCloskey, "The Bourgeois Deal."
19. Ibid, 41, 42.
20. Cf. McCloskey, *The Bourgeois Virtues*, 10.
21. Mumford, *Technics and Civilization*, 102.
22. Scheler, *On Feeling, Knowing, and Valuing*, 120.
23. Carden and McCloskey, "The Bourgeois Deal," 43.
24. McCloskey, *The Bourgeois Virtues*, 34–35.
25. Deirdre McCloskey, "Bourgeois Towns: How Capitalism Became Virtuous, 1600-1776," December 19, 2007, accessed January 15, 2020, https://cadmus.eui.eu/.
26. Keynes, *The General Theory of Employment, Interest, and Money*, 332.
27. Ibid, 333.
28. Abraham H. Maslow, "A Theory of Human Motivation," in *Psychological Review* 50, no. 4 (1943): 370–396.
29. Cf. Mary L. Hirschfeld, *Aquinas and the Market: Toward a Humane Economy* (Cambridge, MA and London: Harvard University Press, 2018), vii.

30. Plato, *Republic,* 175 (Book II).
31. Ibid, 177.
32. Mumford, *Technics and Civilization*, 394.
33. Simone Weil, *L'Enracinement* (Paris: Gallimard, 1949), 53.
34. Mumford, *Technics and Civilization*, 395.
35. Skidelsky and Skidelsky, *How Much is Enough?*, 154–165. These goods are "basic" in the sense that they are deemed "universal," "final," "sui generis" (not part of some other good), and "indispensable." Leisure is not simply free time but instead includes intellectual and volunteering activities. Ibid, 150–152.
36. Ibid, 92.
37. Plato, *Republic II*, 273 (Book VII).
38. Buber, *Pointing the Way*, 221.
39. Heschel, *Who is Man?*, 106.
40. Compare this reasoning with what the Skidelskys write: "There is something else that environmentalists might remember. Prophecies of plague and tempest are a time-honored and yet unlovely way of encouraging a spirit of renunciation. It is kinder (and probably more effective) to show people that a less cluttered life is a good life, one desirable in and of itself." Skidelsky and Skidelsky, *How Much is Enough?*, 125.
41. Augustine, *The City of God. Books I-VII*, 193–194 (Book IV, chapter 3).
42. Rousseau, "Fragments politiques," 529.
43. Ibid, 530.
44. Rousseau, "Lettre à Christophe de Beaumont," 936.
45. See also Opdebeeck, *The Economy and Meaningfulness*, 77–83. Opdebeeck points out the parallels between Rousseau's philosophy and Buddhist philosophy. In chapter five, he elaborates on Rousseau's "third way" between freedom and order.
46. Rousseau, "Émile (Manuscrit Favre)," in *Œuvres complètes de Jean-Jacques Rousseau IV*, 83–84.
47. Rousseau, "Fragments Politiques," 517.
48. Schumacher, *Small is Beautiful*, 28.
49. Ibid, 29.
50. Paul Krugman, "Introduction," in Keynes, *The General Theory of Employment, Interest, and Money*, Xxvii.
51. Ibid.
52. Coyle, *The Economics of Enough*, 186.
53. Strange, *Casino Capitalism*, 29.
54. Coyle, *The Economics of Enough*, 217.
55. Karl Polanyi, "Our Obsolete Market Mentality: Civilization Must Find a New Thought Pattern," *Commentary* 4 (1947): 113.
56. Polanyi, *The Great Transformation*, 76.
57. Coyle, *The Economics of Enough*, 14–15.
58. McCloskey, *The Bourgeois Virtues*, 53.
59. Cf. McCloskey, *The Bourgeois Virtues*, 432.
60. Bourdieu, *The Social Structures of the Economy*, 195. Italics in original text.
61. Hirschfeld, *Aquinas and the Market*, 165.

62. Coyle, *The Economics of Enough*, 213–214.

63. As illustrated by the Libor scandal.

64. Coyle, *The Economics of Enough*, 228–229.

65. Such as Anti-Slavery International, Freedom United, Human Rights Watch, Humanity United, and The Freedom Fund.

66. Sophia Murphy, David Burch, and Jennifer Clapp, "Cereal Secrets: The World's Largest Grain Traders and Global Agriculture," *Oxfam Research Reports*, August 3, 2012, accessed April 30, 2021, https://www.oxfam.org/en/research/cereal-secrets-worlds-largest-grain-traders-and-global-agriculture.

67. Olivier De Schutter, "Addressing Concentration in Food Supply Chains. The Role of Competition Law in Tackling the Abuse of Buyer Power," December 6, 2010, accessed April 30, 2021, https://www.ohchr.org/Documents/Issues/Food/BN3_SRRTF_Competition_ENGLISH.pdf.

68. Schumacher, *Small is Beautiful*, 46.

69. Ibid, 101–102.

70. Arendt, *The Human Condition*, 136.

71. Mumford, *Technics and Civilization*, 391.

72. Arendt, *The Human Condition*, 139.

73. Ibid, 156.

74. Cf. Polanyi, "Our Obsolete Market Mentality," 110.

75. Alina Yohannan, "The Standing Rock Sioux Indians: An Inconvenience for the Black Gold," *Journal of Land and Development* 6 (2016): 19–31; Angie Carter and Ahna Kruzic, "Centering the Commons, Creating Space for the Collective: Ecofeminist# NoDAPL Praxis in Iowa," *Journal of Social Justice* 7 (2017): 1–22; Charles Vlek, "Induced Earthquakes from Long-Term Gas Extraction in Groningen, the Netherlands: Statistical Analysis and Prognosis for Acceptable-Risk Regulation," *Risk Analysis* (2018); Sally Entrekin, Michelle Evans-White, Brent Johnson, and Elisabeth Hagenbuch, "Rapid Expansion of Natural Gas Development Poses a Threat to Surface Waters," *Frontiers in Ecology and the Environment* 9, no. 9 (2011): 503–511.

76. Nigel South and Avi Brisman, "Critical Green Criminology, Environmental Rights and Crimes of Exploitation," *New Directions in Crime and Deviancy* (2013): 99–110, 104.

77. Schumacher, *Small is Beautiful*, 40.

78. It most probably started much earlier since the cultural conditions for the reception of new ideas and practices develop over time.

79. Cf. Taylor, *A Secular Age*, 608–609.

80. Hirschfeld, *Aquinas and the Market*, 5.

81. Bourdieu, *The Social Structures of the Economy*, 227; Coyle, *The Economics of Enough*, 217.

82. Strange, *Casino Capitalism*, 52. More recently, the Skidelskys observe that "the Anglo-American version of individualistic capitalism is kept going largely for the benefit of a predatory plutocracy, whose members cream off the richest prizes while justifying their predation in the language of freedom and globalization. Political leaders continue to enjoy the sound bites of power; the reality is well hidden from

public scrutiny, or even understanding." Skidelsky and Skidelsky, *How Much is Enough?*, 181.

83. Strange, *Casino Capitalism*, 60; Johnson, "The Quiet Coup"; Coyle, *The Economics of Enough*, 256.

84. Keynes, *The General Theory of Employment, Interest, and Money*, 334.

85. Heather Long, "Bernie Sanders Asks If Wall Street is Necessary," *CNN Business*, April 18, 2016, accessed April 30, 2021, https://money.cnn.com/2016/04/18/investing/bernie-sanders-new-york-wall-street/index.html.

86. Strange, *Casino Capitalism*, 38.

87. Keynes, *The General Theory of Employment, Interest, and Money*, 140.

88. Ibid.

89. Skidelsky and Skidelsky, *How Much is Enough?*, 208.

Chapter 5

Coping with Existential Insecurity

EXISTENTIAL MISTRUST

In the previous chapter, I have tried to show that the conceptual and political prioritization of utility and wealth over civic friendship and justice undermines our personal and collective striving for justice. Here I wish to focus on an *attitude* that weakens our love for others and hence for justice, namely, the attitude of existential mistrust, which follows from the existential experience of insecurity. The sense of being trapped in a world organized around injustice, where personal integrity and struggle for justice appear to be drops in an ocean, fuels mistrust, defeatism, cynicism, and resentment. Strange, writing in the 1980s, observed that "only those financial gamblers that still survive in the great office blocks towering over the city centers of the capitalist world will be raising their glasses" to the new millennium.[1] She could not have imagined that two of these tallest towers together with their occupants would become the targets of destructive resentment at the beginning of the twenty-first century. Yet, she did prophetically observe that "frustration and anger become sharper and are apt to be more violently expressed when the realm of luck becomes too large and when the arbitrariness of the system seems to operate so very unequally."[2] As Schumacher and many others before and after him have pointed out, "people who live in highly self-sufficient local communities are less likely to get involved in large-scale violence than people whose existence depends on world-wide systems of trade."[3] The destruction of communities, the deterioration of physical living environments, and soul-destroying work are bound to lead to aggression. These are the various ingredients of uprootedness, which, for Weil, was the source of so many evils.[4] Such uprootedness is not confined to the "losers" in the prevailing socioeconomic jungle. Luc Boltanski and Eve Chiapello speak of "the despair or nihilism which the capitalist order [. . .] constantly induces —not only in those whom it oppresses but also, on occasion, in those who have responsibility for maintaining it, and via education, transmitting its values."[5]

Given the present warlike context, it is both unsurprising and ironic that there have been numerous attempts to restore trust in economic and political institutions.[6] The OECD has repeatedly expressed its concern at the declining trust in governments in several OECD countries. The low level of trust in governments is the main theme of *Government at a Glance 2013*.[7] The authors of that report suggest ways in which governments can win back trust. Six years later, in *Government at a Glance 2019*, people's trust in their government is said to have "recovered back to 45% in the OECD area, a value similar to the pre-crisis level."[8] The report once again emphasizes the need for more people-centered policies and services, and approaches that "allow governments to consult citizens about their needs, encouraging direct participation in designing and implementing policies."[9] Trust has always been the prerequisite for any economic transaction and, of course, for our political cohabitation. The complexity and distance involved in today's economic transactions have made trust even more essential in the modern economy. Yet, trust, similarly to love, is not a disposition that can simply be conjured up. Not only is it difficult to heal a betrayed trust, but it is also unjust to demand from people that they trust that which is untrustworthy. Who would advise their dear ones to walk the streets during a war or to "trust" that they would not be mauled in a jungle full of wolves?

Mutual trust is dependent on our perception of our social environments. It does not fare well in the world of the homo faber, where everything is a means to something else. Given the fact that neoliberalism has been promoting an ethos of every man for himself and sanctioning the survival of the fittest, it seems quite misplaced to speak of trust while the conditions for mistrust are being sustained.[10] That said, it would be unreasonable to blame the prevailing chaos and the resulting general mistrust on the laissez-faire ideology. Laissez-faireism may have reinforced a general climate of mistrust or a siege mentality, but it did not generate that climate or mentality all by itself. As I argued in the previous chapters, the market mentality could only become dominant because a whole culture was receptive to it. That culture is characterized by a particular ontology of the human and the world. The latter is atomistic and thus separative. To judge from the near-universal practice of slavery, the idea of an intrinsic bond that relates human beings has had a hard time in human history. It is thus hardly surprising that it should eventually have lost the battle to the image of individuals as essentially independent beings who sometimes cooperate with each other in order to survive. Similarly, our ambivalent relationship with nature (fear, reverence, and gratitude) has been supplanted by the dualist subject-object relation.

Nature is conceived in such a way that we no longer can relate with it and feel any kinship to it. The homo faber inherits a context in which everything has been despiritualized or desacralized and where the sense of mystery has disappeared. Nothing deserves or arouses our awe and reverence. The cosmos in which we all had a place and a role to play gives way to a universe that now appears "as a sheer and brute accident."[11] We feel ourselves strangers in this world.[12] Blaise Pascal, Buber notes, is the first one in modern times to have expressed the "great anthropological unrest" when he raised the question regarding who the human is in the infinite.[13] Pascal personifies "the new attitude of the person who has become homeless in infinity."[14]

Yet, as Hans Jonas points out,

> There is more to this situation than the mere mood of homelessness, forlornness, and dread. The indifference of nature also means that nature has no reference to ends. With the ejection of teleology from the system of natural causes, nature, itself purposeless, ceased to provide any sanction to possible human purposes. A universe without an intrinsic hierarchy of being, as the Copernican universe is, leaves values ontologically unsupported, and the self is thrown back entirely upon itself in its quest for meaning and value.[15]

Jonas articulates the challenge of nihilism that Nietzsche pointed out. However, the latter did not foresee that existential mistrust would follow from discarding the traditional intuitions about a kindred cosmos. Note that I am not so much referring to the actual, often disputable metaphysical theories about an alleged cosmic order as to the (poetic) images, intuitions, and experiences that are conveyed by these same theories. As I argued in chapter 1, it is possible to reconceive metaphysical and religious traditions as poetry and literature. This might sound insulting to the metaphysician since he might consider metaphysics as an "exact" science. My reply to this possible objection is threefold. For one thing, I am not being derogatory since I believe that poetry and literature are great sources of wisdom; and, for another, in saying that metaphysical and religious legacies have a similar authority as poetry and literature, I am conferring more value on them than they would have had as propositions. My third consideration pertains to the danger of propositions. The latter can be either (temporarily) accepted or rejected. In either case, there is a form of "dogmatism" involved, which might act as an ideological blinder.

In the next pages, I discuss the attitude of existential mistrust, which has been pointed out by Buber and Niebuhr. It refers to the loss of trust in life itself and goes hand in hand with the alienation from reality. I will also suggest ways in which we could overcome it. As I will explain, it is not only a matter of learning a new attitude. Our immediate environments must be reformed in order to foster the experience of existential security. Particular living and working conditions reinforce the alienation from reality by creating separate worlds in which people are either cogs in a machine or (un)willing players in a "virtual reality."[16] It is noteworthy that Lasch, in an interview a few months before he died, refers to the basic trust in life as "hope." He says:

> Hope, on the other hand, isn't tied to a vision of the future. It's more like what Erik Erikson and other psychoanalysts mean when they talk about "basic trust." It's a trusting attitude toward life, as opposed to the attitude of mistrust and resentment and despair that so many of us carry around with us.[17]

Accordingly, the trust in life does not involve a particular conception of the world or the belief that the world is the best of all possible worlds. Instead, it is the trust that underpins all our human actions and endeavors, from crawling to caring. As I will be showing, we do not need to endorse explicit doctrines or ideas to regain some kind of trust in life and in each other. In fact, I think that Nietzsche, despite his criticism of rationalism, might have overestimated the role of explicit ideas and beliefs in human life. The basic trust in life is transmitted from parent to child and sustained through the practices of dialogic life. The metaphysical idea of a pregiven cosmic order may be hard to prove (and may be unprovable), but those who partake in the life of dialogue experience that love is stronger than self-interest.[18]

PRIMARY RELIGION

In the previous chapter, I have pointed out that not all wants are equal and that the ordering of desires is a precondition for the unification of the self. The few examples that I provided illustrated the variety of hierarchies of needs (desires) that follows from the diversity inherent in humankind. However, there are certain needs that can be considered higher for all humans, irrespective of our particular vocations. "Security" is of one of them. Security is a complex concept and phenomenon, referring to both physical and psychical security. Like the need for order and freedom, the need for security can be excessively intensified. As a result, the striving for security expresses itself not only in the demand for "security and peace and social equilibrium, but [also in] a striving to express power over the environment, a goal of dominance over one's fellows."[19] That excessive striving for security manifests itself in conquests but also in the limitless accumulation of wealth and material goods and the building of walls and fortresses. A perpetually uncertain environment can partly explain this insatiable desire for security, which becomes a desire for power to compensate for the feeling of insecurity. In his *Afterword* to Keynes' *The General Theory of Employment, Interest, and Money* (2018), Robert Skidelsky underscores the important role that uncertainty plays in Keynes' theory. Money is a hedge against the uncertainty of the future.[20] The symbolic value of money, however, should not be underestimated. Alfred Alder mentions a case to illustrate his argument that money is associated with power:

> One of those very wealthy men who, although he should have had quite enough, continued to chase after money, admitted after the beginning of a delusional insanity: "Yes, do you know that (money) is the power which constantly allures me again and again!" This man understood it, but many dare not understand it.[21]

Similarly, Niebuhr notes that these "vast metropolitan conglomerates of ours [. . .] are monstrosities from an economic standpoint. They are built for psychological reasons."[22] They compensate for our feelings of vulnerability and insignificance in an indifferent universe.

These same psychological reasons seem to be behind the reluctance to give up the narratives of growth and progress. They may also explain the faith that "technology" will make it possible to continue along the same traditional path. Fear of the unknown is human but so too is justice. Some might argue that fear and selfishness are more natural to the human than justice is. Yet, the proof that we are capable of justice is provided time and again when we are able to overcome our natural fear and selfishness for the sake of our loved ones and our country. For sure, being just and unselfish is much more of a struggle than fearfully clinging on to our old habits and familiar world. This brings me back to my question regarding that which can help us in our struggle to overcome our siege mentality. I suggested in the introduction that the antidote to existential mistrust is what the ancients called "piety" and what Niebuhr calls "primary religion."[23] "Piety" and "primary religion" are not equivalent, but they both convey a similar attitude of reverence toward all that which deserves our gratitude, admiration, or respect. My focus here is on the attitude of reverence and not so much on the object, which may be our parents, country, God (or gods), or nature. Reverence involves love and perhaps a certain degree of self-effacement, which is another word for humility. Such an attitude is an antidote to the instrumental mentality of the homo faber and the indifference of the purportedly "impartial" observer (or spectator). When we (momentarily) feel reverence for the mystery of life or of nature, we refuse to dissect and divide it into categories. This is when we may realize that reality transcends our understanding.

In Cicero's well-known Dream of Scipio, Scipio Africanus the Elder tells his grandson that he must cultivate justice and piety, not only with respect to his parents and relatives but also toward his fatherland and the whole Earth.[24]

Like in Plato's Myth of Er, the brave men who fight for their fatherland are promised a privileged place in heaven. There is no need to fear death. Cicero delves slightly more elaborately into the cosmology that underpins ancient humanism. The whole universe is presented as being ruled by a god who loves justice and who takes delight in justice among human beings.[25] The beauty and harmony of the cosmos is revealed to Scipio Africanus the Younger. When the latter expresses his wish to be with his grandfather and thus sees no reason not to hasten his departure to heaven, Scipio Africanus the Elder replies:

> Human beings have been begotten under this law: that they may protect that globe you see in the middle of this sacred zone, which is called Earth. And a soul has been given to them from those everlasting fires that you call stars and planets, which are spherical and round, animated with divine minds, and which accomplish their circles and orbs with marvelous swiftness. Therefore, Publius, you and all pious persons must keep your souls in the custody of your bodies, and you must not depart from human life without the order of him by whom your soul has been given to you, so that you will not seem to flee the human task assigned by the god.[26]

It is noteworthy that Cicero, similarly to Marcus Aurelius, goes to great lengths to defend the philosophical perspective that the universe is governed by a just and intelligent power (god). Therefore, the world deserves our efforts and sacrifice.

We may not wish to endorse Cicero's cosmology, but we may be able to recognize that it is psychologically hard to accept moral responsibility for a world that is devoid of an intrinsic moral order. In a world in which survival seems to be the only rule, I may be able to accept responsibility for my loved ones, but my motivation to sacrifice my interests for strangers will be weak. There is nothing that intrinsically relates me to them, just as nothing relates me to the polar bear in the Arctic. There is no compelling reason for me to be just at the expense of my own interests when I know that everyone else is driven by his own selfish interests. When we say that the world is devoid of order, we mean that "justice," "injustice," or "fraternity" are essentially empty words to which we (as individuals and collectivities) choose to attribute significance. We "invent" these values to make cohabitation possible. On a side note, the idea that we can create authoritative values and imprint them on a neutral reality is as absurd as the idea that an indifferent nature can generate creative beings who have the capacity to care.[27] Most of us do not live beyond good and evil and thus do not consider ideals such as justice and fraternity as the arbitrary inventions of our ancestors, which we can choose to dismiss if we wish to. In a strong sense, we cannot help being "moral," in the sense of being thinking, judging, and caring beings, even if we sometimes have the wrong commitment.[28] Dehumanization consists in losing these capacities.

Even in more or less normal situations, our moral vigor does wane in the face of the apparent futility of all our endeavors and struggles. As Niebuhr writes,

> Human vitality has two primary sources, animal impulse and confidence in the meaningfulness of human existence. The more human consciousness arises to full self-consciousness and to a complete recognition of the total forces of the universe in which it finds itself, the more it requires not only animal vitality but confidence in the meaningfulness of its world to maintain a healthy will-to-live. This confidence in the meaningfulness of life is not something which results from a sophisticated analysis of the forces and factors which surround the human enterprise. It is something which is assumed in every healthy life. It is primary religion. Men may be quite unable to define the meaning of life, and yet live it by a simple trust that is meaning. This primary religion is the basic optimism of all vital and wholesome human life.[29]

Existential mistrust means that we have somehow lost this basic "optimism" and are failing to come to terms with life. One would indeed be hard-pressed to discern any unity or meaning in a world marked by intense competition, casualization of the workforce, fragile relationships, and lack of solidarity. In this context, our will to live turns into the will to power.

A basic trust or optimism is basic in the same sense as a first principle is first. It cannot be proven. Myths, religions, and philosophical traditions try to articulate reasons for piety or that basic trust, but these "reasons" are no proofs. Any conceived metaphysical, philosophical, or scientific unity does not provide the experience of organic unity, which is the precondition for meaning. Similarly, the ultimate trust in life or the world is not based on the perception of harmony in the world. It is instead transmitted in genuine human communities, which are "genuine" by virtue of their capacity for being "food" for individual souls. That notion of a community as "food," which I owe to Weil, is useful to counter the biggest danger inherent to all social bodies, namely, collective egoism. Food is essential to survival, but it is normally not worshipped. Weil thus holds that a collectivity does not deserve more esteem than food. Love, she writes, is due only to the universe, with the "totality of reasonable creatures that it has contained, contains and will contain."[30] All other human communities, such as our families, tribes, countries, and religious communities, demand our commitments and even sacrifices but not our unconditional love. We owe respect to communities because they root individual souls without melting them into an anonymous mass. Rooting, according to Weil, is perhaps the most important and yet unknown need of the human soul. Communities bring human souls in contact "with nature, the past, tradition."[31] They provide a certain permanence and hence finality to human life by preserving "particular treasures of the past and presentiments of the future."[32] Uprooting thus takes place when the past and future of people are destroyed. Colonialism, imperialism, and globalism have such destructive effects. Counterreactions, unfortunately enough, often do not restore what has been lost because they are often motivated by revenge, which Weil considered to be "the worst of finalities."[33] The original uprooting creates a vicious circle that can only be broken if the desire for justice is positively motivated and not negatively motivated by resentment.

Piety and primary religion presume communities whose traditions are partly informed by myths, religious beliefs, and intuitions. Notwithstanding the disputable nature of some beliefs, religions do have the potential to enable their adherents to come to terms with their universe by cultivating "poetic insight and moral vigor."[34] Religions, being the human expressions of the conceived relationship between the human and God (or gods), are not exempt from the human tendency to create "false eternals."[35] As Buber notes, "the historical religions have the tendency to become ends in themselves and, as it were, to put themselves in God's place, and, in fact, there is nothing that is so apt to obscure the face of God as a religion."[36] If religions give up their claims to absolute truth and exclusivism, they can promote the search for higher forms of justice, the expansion of existing loyalties and the cultivation of the "attitude of both filial piety and heroic rebellion" toward the universe.[37] What about the nonreligious among us? This question is especially relevant to readers who have inherited Western modernity's distinction between the religious and the secular. It is quite irrelevant to those who are still rooted in communities since individual religious beliefs or nonbeliefs do not matter much in the common struggle for justice. In fact, it could even be argued that no one who is driven by the love for strangers and the sacred desire for justice can be called nonreligious.[38] She can be considered as deeply pious or manifests what the Skidelskys refer to as a "religious impulse" in the concluding part of their book. They doubt whether "a society entirely devoid of the religious impulse [could] stir itself to the pursuit of the common good."[39]

WORK ENDOWED WITH FINALITY

Given the fact that work constitutes a substantial part of our human existence, it is hardly surprising that our work reality should influence our perception of life and our fellow beings. The nature and conditions of our work can foster existential mistrust by alienating us from the totality of life and other beings.

Certain experiences can make us believe that humans are not to be trusted because they are primarily motivated by their narrow selfish interests. Those endless hours behind a computer screen filled with data and charts can numb our souls. The challenge is therefore to make positive use of that pervasive power of work so that the latter can be made to play its part in the humanization of economic and human life. Dialogic life is a possibility in work contexts too. This may sound absurd or hopelessly "idealistic" but only because we do not seem to be able to move away from our "economy of acquisition" to an "economy of need."[40] Societies were not always consumer societies and work was not always the means to consume or to happiness.[41] The collapse of the social body in early modern times and the corresponding disembedding of the economy from social relationships have resulted in a new approach to people and work. The emphasis on gain and growth, on productivity and efficiency have led to satanic mills worldwide. Working conditions have somewhat improved in the more "developed" parts of the world and in particular sectors where the interests of workers are defended by collective labor/bargaining agreements.[42] The health and safety of workers have gained attention largely because of trade unions' actions and legal coercion. This also means that those who are not protected by collective labor agreements and legal regulations still run the risk of being exploited and exposed to health hazards. Dire working conditions are still common in many parts of the world, where products for the richer countries are produced. We are thus all still directly and indirectly involved in the exploitation of fellow beings. In order to end this vicious circle, we must break with tradition.

The "utilitarian outlook" to which we have been forcefully converted undermines dialogic life or civic friendship.[43] In this context, it is difficult to see whether we are perpetrators or victims of injustice since, as Polanyi points out, we are forced to act on what have become "economic motives"—that is, hunger and gain—"under pain of being trodden under foot by the juggernaut market."[44] We are all subjected to the economic necessity of "earning a living." Having and getting a "job" that pays well is a matter of life and death in our present context. To borrow Arendt's insightful distinction, work has turned into labor, but differently from labor in the pre-market economy, our work is devoid of the "blessing of labor," which consists in the gratification that follows our efforts.[45] That blessing, Arendt observes, should not be confused with "the inevitably brief spell of relief and joy which follows accomplishment and attends achievement."[46] In other words, most of us can neither take joy in the products of our hands (homo faber)—because we do not make them—nor enjoy the fruits of our efforts (animal laborans).[47] The transformation of work into labor implies that we are constantly under the yoke of economic necessity, which most of us cannot escape. The anti-social and anti-civilizational nature of this condition becomes clearer when we realize that a human civilization is meant to protect individual persons from natural necessity and hence from the threat of "individual destitution."[48] Economic misery, in contrast to poverty, is peculiar to a market-dominated society where individuals are no longer members of a community and therefore have to fend for themselves. Charles Péguy aptly remarks that the very fact that such economic misery exists means that there is no city, no human society at all. Economic misery, he writes, dehumanizes the destitute, making them worse than slaves.[49] The *misérables* can only think of bread and becoming rich in order to leave that state of destitution. They are excluded from the life of a human community.

Primitive economies were in a sense more humane because they were organized in such a way that no individual had to fear starvation as long as there were collective resources.[50] Individual efforts, through work and labor, were directed toward securing collective goods (both material and nonmaterial), which were then distributed among members. The differences in the original contributions were not taken into account. Of course, this is similar to how things work in a healthy family. Without wishing to romanticize past communities to which we no longer have access, I think that it is instructive to examine why and how work and labor in these pre-market economy contexts were more humane. I would like to mention six aspects here. One is the direct relation between the efforts of individual persons and collective goods. It is easier for members of the community to see how their activities contribute to goods that sustain the lives of all because division of labor and specialization are much more limited. Related to this is the nature of the collective goods. They are necessary and useful goods, including nonmaterial goods that foster a good human life (such as music, paintings, poetry, and stories). A third aspect is the variety of activities performed by a person. A fourth feature is of course the embeddedness of these activities in a community. Even such a boring task as peeling peanuts is made more pleasant through conversations, stories, or singing. The same person will be doing different other tasks during the day, such as cooking, making clothes, cleaning, and taking care of her children. This brings me to two other features, namely, time and space. There is no external time pressure since the absurd idea that time is money is absent. Yet, things get done because the subsistence of a whole community depends on devoted members. There is more physical freedom and contact with total reality since the space in which a particular activity is performed is not essentially different from the living space, while labor takes place in the open air.

Work and labor in pre-capitalist, post-capitalist, and noncapitalist contexts are not necessarily "meaningful." In fact, it is dubious whether the question of meaning—whether life and work are meaningful or meaningless—arises at all. Labor is not necessarily the source of happiness or self-fulfillment. Yet, it is endowed with finality because it is embedded in a human community that is a community by virtue of its justice and fraternity. The expression "work endowed with finality," which I again owe to Weil, is arguably more appropriate than "meaningful work." The experience of finality is that of plenitude, which makes it unnecessary to seek a reason to live and to work.[51] Such finality clearly depends both on the nature of work and its cultural context. The more work is related to the real needs of people, the greater the unity between work and human existence. Such coherence is painfully absent in our present context. It should by now be clear that most types of work today are devoid of finality. The same task, for instance, peeling of peanuts—or even more topical, shrimps—in an industrial context becomes a dehumanizing, soul-numbing activity.[52] The instrumental mentality manifests itself to its fullest in the factory environment, which, despite being safer and cleaner, are still unfit for humans. Though there are differences between factories in the developed parts of the world and those in the poorer parts of the world, these differences are of degree rather than of kind. The features of work or labor that make it a human activity are absent in a factory milieu. Time and space are strictly regulated. The physical arrangement of a factory serves the aims of order (and hence control), efficiency, and productivity.[53] Correspondingly, unproductive and disruptive activities such as talking and laughing are discouraged. Even the access to sanitary facilities is strongly monitored and, in some cases, denied.[54] The maximum must be squeezed out of every individual, who is replaced by another if he (she) does not work quickly enough. This obsession with productivity and efficiency is odd given the fact that so many overproduced goods are constantly being destroyed.[55]

Even more fundamentally, however, the willingness to treat fellow beings as disposable objects is stupefying. Some may wish to blame this attitude on "the market," that is, on the economic necessity to keep production costs below market prices. However, it might be more accurate to blame the game of the market (stronger players trying to annihilate weaker ones) on the will to power, gain, and domination. In this sense, those who are incapable of treating their fellow workers as their equals are essentially not different from slaveholders, slave traders, and human traffickers. At a more subtle level, the incapacity or refusal to acknowledge the destructive effects of repetitive and boring activities manifests the contempt for the human body and spirit. The disembeddedness of work from its social environment and the corresponding uprooting of workers are most manifest in factories. However, offices, shops, and other workplaces do not necessarily escape the instrumental logic, constant monitoring, and performance pressure. The fact that economic activities harm the very people whom they are meant to serve reveals the untenable contradiction in the present organization of work. In a people-centered economy of needs, the quality of work and its effects on the human body spirit and its further consequences must be considered. As Mumford writes:

> Our disregard for the quality of work itself, for work as a vital and educational process, is so habitual that it scarcely ever enters into our social demands. Yet it is plain that in the decision as to whether to build a bridge or a tunnel there is a human question that should outweigh the question of cheapness or mechanical feasibility: namely, the number of lives that will be lost in the actual building or the advisability of condemning a certain number of men to spend their entire working days underground supervising tunnel traffic. As soon as our thought ceases to be automatically conditioned by the mine, such questions become important.[56]

Work conceived this way is not merely the means to consumption and thus an inescapable evil for many. It becomes a thoroughly human activity that is socializing and humanizing.

More wholesome forms of work, more freedom, more genuine human contact, and less automatism do not necessarily mean higher costs. Moreover, once we do take the needs of people seriously, including those of workers, we are bound to evaluate technology differently. We have been made to believe that productivity (as well as efficiency) increases with more technology (automation) and less labor. However, this is a fallacious belief that rests on a miscalculation of the real price of technology. The real price will have to include fair wages and humane working conditions for *all* those involved in the production chain of that particular technology, including for the suppliers of raw materials, all possible present and future externalities (including the effects of raw materials extraction), and the real costs of disposal/product destruction.[57] The same calculation must be made with respect to all other complementary goods that are necessary for the functioning of that particular technology. In the case of energy, it is obvious that nonrenewables are simply priceless. Most of us are aware that the market price of technology is relatively low—low enough to be affordable—because of exploitation especially at the bottom of the production chain and private appropriation of commons (water, gas, oil, and land). We may be less aware of the fact that it is also low because businesses and states are able to make the larger community (national and global, present and future generations) bear the costs of disposal (dumping on land and in water) and externalities (air and water pollution).[58] In other words, a labor and time-intensive production process is not necessarily more expensive. This does not mean that labor should be "cheap." The question of just, living wages is certainly part of better working conditions but deserves much more attention than I can give to it here. In any case, it is far too an important matter to be left to market forces that are not bound to the social values of a human civilization.

The conception of work as a human, creative and educational process implies less specialization, less order (and less corseting), and less control.

Less specialization also means that we must rethink the prevalent forms of division of labor. Cleaning and housekeeping are officially jobs, but we may wish to reconsider whether such specialization is morally just. It is one thing to *be* a carpenter, but it is quite another to *be* a cleaner day in day out. Moreover, it is remarkable that the activities that most of us like the least (such as dish-washing, laundry, cleaning, and waste collection) and gladly outsource are the lowest paid jobs. It could be argued that any activity that could be done by a robot ought not to become the principal and sole activity (the "job") of a person. Instead, such activity can be part of a more comprehensive range of responsibilities that involve social interaction and creativity. The so-called "unskilled" workers can get a further on-the-job training and a general human cultivation that makes them experience the life of a genuine human community. Till now, some of us have tried to escape the more tedious aspects of work by getting the socially weak—typically slaves, women, Blacks, migrant workers, and the "unskilled"—to carry out the menial and cumbersome tasks. Fairness requires that these tasks be more equally distributed and no longer isolated from more creative tasks. Only then will work become more humane and less alienating for all. The unwillingness to revise our current practices, division of labor, and hierarchy of skills/values would reflect the absence of a democratic aspiration to justice and civic friendship. It would also reflect our incapacity to break with the undemocratic tradition of forcing particular classes to cater to the comfort and pleasures of privileged classes.

The humanization of work and workplaces also means that we—as a political community—must review existing and emerging industries. Do they serve the real needs of people today and tomorrow? What are their real prices? Does work in these industries foster the general well-being of humans and preserve their unity with their natural and social environments? Sisyphean types of work must be endowed with finality since they are "an insult to human nature [and] which must necessarily and inevitably produce either escapism or aggression, and that no amount of '"bread and circuses' can compensate for the damage done."[59] Perhaps even more fundamentally, the "worth" of people should be detached from economic activities and achievements, especially paid employment. This means that self-fulfillment should no longer be regarded as being dependent on our economic position or "productivity." Such a cultural revolution is undeniably easier said than done. The ideas of humanity and human dignity (and more recently, human rights) have not been powerful (or "real" enough) to counter slavery, racism, misogyny, and exploitation in general. Ideas are impotent if they are not embodied in daily practices. The radical transformation of work is therefore not possible without the political and corporate commitment to the common good. An exceptionally strong political will be necessary to limit the power of the market and check the size of corporations; to stimulate certain industries and discourage others; and protect individuals from "economic necessity." Regarding corporate leaders, Buber believed that they would be able to "practise the responsibility of dialogue."[60] Let us hope that they are indeed able to accept the responsibility for their fellow beings and the world and resist the urge to self-aggrandizement and profit at any price.

TRUSTWORTHY LEADERSHIP

Various scholars and observers have pointed out a crisis of legitimacy or a general crisis of governance. Peoples, worldwide, have lost trust in their political elites, as documented by several OECD publications.[61] The need for a "people-centric" and "inclusive" approach is repeatedly emphasized in these writings. In other words, a democratic government ought to represent a whole people. Its policies ought to protect and foster the values constitutive of a democracy, namely, justice, equality, and fraternity. Governments are no longer trusted precisely because they have failed and are still failing to "control the dominant economic forces and subordinate them to genuinely universal ends."[62] Instead, they are what Buber calls "pseudo-representatives of amorphous masses of electors."[63] Is such failure to be blamed on weakness or an unhealthy alliance with corporate power? Both, most probably. Laissez-faire government policies automatically promote the interests of particular parties, as opposed to a whole people. The political elite benefits from the present condition, as revealed by the Panama Papers. The extent to which the contemporary political elite has drifted away from the democratic ideal is disconcerting. At the same time, as I have noted in the previous chapters, governments have lost their power to private powers. "Governance" can no longer be equated with national governments but instead comprises the influence of many more actors that are not necessarily committed to the common good (or universal ends). The elites, as Lasch writes, are "those who control the international flow of money and information, preside over philanthropic foundations and institutions of higher learning, manage the instruments of cultural production and thus set the terms of public debate."[64] Such power must be directed to the common good if we are to regain trust in our social existence and eventually in human life itself. This means that we must demand and expect our elites to be trustworthy above all things.

In his *De Re Publica*, through the mouthpiece of Scipio Africanus, Cicero defines the republic as the *res* ("thing") of the people, emphasizing that the people is not "every assemblage of human beings herded together in whatever way, but an assemblage of a multitude united in agreement about right and in the sharing of advantage."[65] Differently from Socrates in Plato's *Politeia*, Cicero observes that the people does not arise through mutual needs or weakness but instead because of the natural sociability of the human species. Elsewhere, he writes that both the love (*amor*) and friendship (*amicitia*) that bind people originate in nature and do not arise out of need.[66] In other words, we do not love and interact with each other because we must cooperate to survive (that is, for utilitarian reasons) but because we are made for love and justice.[67] In the ideal city-state, citizens are virtuous and relate to each other in justice. A person is virtuous when judgement or wisdom (*consilio*)—the best part of the mind—commands. There is then no place for avarice, the desire for power and glory, and lusts.[68] Instead, modesty, temperance, self-control, a sense of shame, decency, and chastity are the fruits of right judgement and right reason.[69] Whether Rome was ever such a republic or not does not matter right now. The troublesome facts that such an ideal Republic depended on slaves and went hand in hand with a strict social stratification must also be left aside. What is here relevant is that Cicero blames the degeneration of the city-state on the corruption of the political elite, which in turn corrupts the public opinion and hence the mores of a people. Hence, he notes that the city-state disintegrated due to the wrong opinion regarding the ends of human life.

By means of the dialogue between Scipio Africanus and his friends, Cicero explains that the ideal Republic—which combines and hence moderates the monarchical, aristocratic and popular forms of Republic—fell into decadence when good leadership became associated with wealth or family name (nobility of descent).[70] As a result, the leadership of the city-state got into the hands of either the rich or the noble of name, irrespective of whether they were virtuous or not.[71] Since Cicero believes in the power of good and bad examples, he considers bad leadership to be extremely infectious:

> Vicious leading men behave more ruinously toward the republic because they not only sow their own vices but also instill them into the city. Not only are they a hindrance by being corrupted themselves, but also, by corrupting others, they do more harm by example than by fault.[72]

The corrupted ideas and practices of the elite affect the customs prevailing in a society. By losing trust in those whom we believe capable of justice and wisdom and of acting accordingly, we also lose trust in the future. The distrust of authorities affects our self-understanding, our perception of others and instils doubts about the goodness of our worldly life. If leaders repeatedly betray our trust, mistrust turns into cynicism. Moral ideals and values become less credible and become empty slogans. Such a condition is not easily reversed. Consequently, even the most exemplary leaders will find it subsequently difficult to counter the nihilism that ensued from bad leadership. In this sense, it would be simplistic to claim that trustworthy leaders can save a corrupted world. Both ancient and modern thinkers remind us that an ounce of prevention is worth a pound of cure. Corrupted habits of the heart and mind are difficult to heal. Exceptionally charismatic leaders can be inspiring and lift the spirits of a people, but unless they have the power to bring about structural changes, their influence will be short-lived.

Once elites realize that their decisions affect a whole world today and tomorrow, they may wish to consider and carry their mighty responsibilities. Once again, we can turn to the eloquence of Cicero for a description of the duties of those holding the power to influence our lives. He thus writes:

> The administration of a commonwealth is like a guardianship: it must be conducted for the utility of those whom have been entrusted to your care, not for those to whom it was entrusted. On the other hand, those who take into consideration the interests of a part of the citizenry and neglect another introduce a most pernicious thing into a political community: sedition and discord. The result is that some are seen as being attached to the multitude, others as adherents of the best people, and few as devoted to everyone. [. . .] A serious and courageous citizen worthy of pre-eminence in the commonwealth will avoid and hate these things. He will surrender himself completely to the commonwealth, and will pursue neither influence nor power; instead, he will protect the whole commonwealth so as to take into consideration the interests of everyone.[73]

It seems obvious that the representatives of a people must be committed to the interests of all. It is also clear that political leaders failed to live up to that promise in Cicero's time and have blatantly failed to do so in our time too. Our situation is even more complicated. For one thing, because power is not only in the hands of chosen representatives and, for another, because of our divided societies (or more precisely, the absence of society or a political community).

The gap between certain groups of people and the political elite has been frequently pointed out, also by the OECD. Political representatives have been accused of serving particular interests (such as those of particular industries) as opposed to universal ends. Policies often reflect this bias and hence also the fear of displeasing the actors that politics has been serving. This subservience of the political to the economic is of course the consequence of economism. As long as the passion for wealth, welfare, and comfort is the most powerful passion, such monstrous relation will be maintained. If the chosen political elite truly wish to be the representative of all people, then they ought to become aware of the ends of human life that are the most appropriate to humans. This means acknowledging the nonnaturalistic conceptions of who humans are and the hierarchies of values that correspond to these conceptions. The impossible challenge that arises once we acknowledge the clash between different philosophical anthropologies, namely the political need to reconcile the different hierarchies of values, has always been there but has simply been ignored by opting for naturalistic materialism. For the present purpose, the challenge can be limited to the political choices between on the one hand, justice and civic friendship, and on the other hand, utility and self-reliance. The clash between justice and utility, as I have shown in the previous chapter, is a permanent one. The modern solution to the conflict has consisted in giving priority to utility. Such a choice is in accordance with the separative model of human nature. The same holds for the emphasis on self-reliance. The separative or contractual model of human nature, as I have argued earlier, is the least suitable to sustaining a society. Justice and civic friendship, which constitute the "glue" of society, require a richer account of who we are and of the nature of our relationships. We need not adhere to so-called comprehensive doctrines to realize that the *après moi, le déluge* mentality in politics is thoroughly irresponsible.

It is significant that Cicero emphasizes the importance of justice in good leaders, while we are inclined to think in terms of political skills (such as the ability to negotiate) and slightly more broadly, in terms of political prudence or wisdom. Yet, prudence without justice is a pseudo-prudence. The clever and cunning politician does not inspire much trust. Cicero thus writes:

> Now being considered trustworthy can be achieved from two things: if we are believed to have attained prudence combined with justice. For we consider those trustworthy whom we think understand more than ourselves, whom we believe can foresee future events, and, when something occurs and has become a crisis, can sort out and resolve the matter according to the circumstances—such is the prudence human beings believe useful and true. But trust is placed in just human beings—that is to say, good men—because there is no suspicion of fraud or injury about them. And so we quite correctly entrust to them our safety, to them our fortunes, to them our children. Of the two, then, justice is better able to establish trust, insofar as it has sufficient authority without prudence, while prudence is entirely incapable of establishing trust without justice.[74]

This is a slightly different way of recalling the unity of virtues, which, as Cicero shows, is not simply a theory but is confirmed by experience. Such a unity of virtues is indispensable in those to whom we have entrusted our lives and those of future generations. They are expected to have unified their souls before they take important decisions and should "have the power to replenish and renew themselves in a manner conformable to their task."[75] Trustworthy leaders must therefore not only be well trained and skilled but, above all things, must be virtuous. The tendency to disregard the character of our political leaders and their private lives (as well as their writings) reflects a distorted view of politics. Politics is not a technical affair, and there is no method for good political decisions. Whoever partake in politics allow their justice (unified soul) or injustice (broken soul) to inform their political decisions.

This ancient humanist approach to leadership, in which the care of the soul and the cultivation of virtuous citizens are core features, has been creatively re-appropriated by Fénelon and Rousseau. The latter's pedagogical writings reflect the influence of the former. The difference between these two men and Machiavelli, for instance (who is also heir to the ancient humanist and republican tradition), precisely lies in their different ideas of great leadership. In Fénelon and Rousseau, the influence of the "gentle" and devirilizing effect of Christianity is visible. That said, it could be argued that there has always been that gentle and devirilizing tendency among ancient writers as well. While this certainly holds for poets, that "gentleness" is expressed by Cicero when he notes that "although most people think that martial affairs are greater than urbane ones, this opinion must be curtailed."[76] He explains that many warriors long for glory, whereas those who devote themselves to public affairs do so because they are genuinely committed to the res publica. Rousseau, similarly, succeeds in merging the traditional virtue of self-mastery with the "gentler" virtues of tenderness, compassion, and humility. Hence, though Lycurgus and Cato were virtuous in the first sense, they were also virtuous in the second sense.[77] Rousseau praises Lycurgus for abdicating the throne and giving it back to the legitimate ruler. Cato is remembered for creating a society of virtuous citizens. In his eulogy of the Duke of Orléans (1703–1752), Rousseau praises the erudition, piety, and charity of the man who was also known as Louis the Pious.[78] Great leaders must have enjoyed a liberal arts education and be fully acquainted with their own strengths and weaknesses. They learn about virtues in books and practice them in the fulfilment of their duties. Leaders must cultivate the discernment necessary to distinguish between genuine friends-advisors and self-interested deceivers.

I would like to conclude this section by bringing in a fascinating work of Fénelon, namely, *Les aventures de Télémaque, fils d'Ulysse* (The Adventures of Telemachus, the Son of Ulysses). That novel was written with the aim of educating the future king of France and is thus certainly of great value to any leader today as well.[79] François de Salignac de La Mothe-Fénelon was the tutor of the Duke of Burgundy, Louis XIV's grandson. The duke, it is reported, was not an easy pupil. The seven-year-old young prince was prone to fits of rage and was haughty.[80] Fénelon's patience and love appear to have borne fruit. The young prince became a pious young man and conscious of his responsibilities as a future king, quite the opposite of his grandfather.[81] At a later stage of the story, Mentor (who is the goddess Minerva in disguise), the tutor of Telemachus, expresses his joy at the personal growth of his pupil. Mentor says:

> You were by nature hard-hearted and haughty; your heart was moved only by your comforts and interests; but you have finally become human, and you begin, by the experience of your miseries, to commiserate with those of others. Without this compassion, one has neither kindness, nor virtue, nor the capacity to govern humans.[82]

In the last book of the novel, Fénelon summarizes the qualities of a trustworthy leader. Mentor is about to leave his protégé after having guided him for several years and finally reveals himself as Minerva. In her concluding speech, Minerva summarizes what she has taught Telemachus during the years they spent together:

> Love the peoples; spare no effort to gain their love [. . .] Eschew effeminacy [*la mollesse*], splendour, excesses; take pride in simplicity; let your virtues and your good actions be the ornaments of your person and palace [. . .]; never forget that kings do not reign for their own glory but for the good of their peoples [. . .] Above all, beware of your temper and caprice: it is an enemy that you will take everywhere with you till death; it will intrude into your counsels and betray you if you listen to its suggestions.
>
> [. . .] Fear the gods, O Telemachus; this fear is the greatest treasure of the human heart: with it will come wisdom, justice, peace, joy, genuine pleasures, true liberty, simple abundance, untarnished glory.[83]

The notion of the fear of gods recurs throughout the whole novel and is comparable to what I have referred to as piety or primary religion above. Phrased slightly differently, it means that those who hold power are to be conscious of their dependence on a wisdom that they do not possess but of which they can partake if they are willing to see themselves as *serving* those in their charge.

THE CREATION OF ORGANIC UNITY

Good leadership can re-humanize our working and living environments, thereby mitigating the sense of insecurity. However, politics by itself cannot heal our broken relationships with our fellow beings and cannot help us to be at home in our universe. We need renewed vitality and courage—or, in Niebuhr's words, "poetic insight and moral vigor"—to confront the insecurity that is inherent to life. Such vital and moral energy is cultivated in the security of genuine human communities, which have precisely been destroyed. The impersonalism of industrial societies and unbridled economic power have done much harm that cannot be easily undone. In this context of survivalism, communities are replaced by narrow and unilateral commitments, which are often endowed with the aura of universalism and absolutism. What we need is a sense of connectedness that transcends our divisions and fears. That sense of connectedness cannot be ideological or technological. We have more than enough of these kinds of false unities and identities. Instead, we must re-organize our lives in accordance with the higher values of brotherhood and sisterhood. As Mumford writes,

> Ideas of humanity come, so to say, from other parts of the environment [as opposed to science and technics]: the herdsman or the caravaneer brooding under the stars—a Moses, a David, a St. Paul—or the city bred man, observing closely the conditions under which men may live well together—a Confucius, a Socrates, a Jesus, bring into society the notions of peace and friendly cooperation as a higher moral expression than the subjection of other men. Often this feeling, as in St. Francis and the Hindu sages, extends to the entire world of living nature.[84]

In other words, we do not need to invent new notions of fellowship, values, and ideals. They are readily available. We simply need to creatively re-appropriate them in our new historical contexts and allow them to be our sources of inspiration in our concrete lives.

It can sound counterintuitive to suggest that organic unity can be *created*. Can a sense of fellowship or dialogic life be created? In certain ways, yes. Such creation involves both passive and active elements, including the shaping of the conditions for such fellowship. A vital condition is of course justice. There can be no genuine unity without a just order. This means that justice must be prioritized, politically and institutionally. Niebuhr thus notes:

> To accomplish this purpose some of our own preconceptions must go and the same law of love which is no simple possibility for man or society must be enthroned as yet the final standard of every institution, structure and system of justice. To those who exalt freedom we must declare that freedom without community is not love but leads to man making himself his own end. [. . .] To those who fear the extension of the state for the regulation of modern economic life we must point out that their fears are frequently prompted not by a concern for justice but by a jealous desire to maintain their own power.[85]

The prioritization of justice necessarily entails an economy of needs. The failure to limit our needs leads to strife since we all want the same or what others have. Unlimited desires are not compatible with the boundaries of the material world. Moreover, since justice means attributing the same weight to the interests of future generations, we must regain a notion of enough.

Psychologically and spiritually speaking, unlimited desires reflect a disordered soul. Since justice is in the first place personal and interpersonal justice, disordered souls result in injustice at the collective level. Another precondition for fellowship is of course an increased openness to the other. In other words, we must learn to love the stranger and include him (her) in our immediate circles. The (Augustinian) idea of the expansion of one's love, commitment or loyalty is relevant to this purpose. According to this perspective, conflicts and clashing partial interests, in both political and economic realms, can be transcended by moving to a higher plane. This means that compromises between conflicting claims can be reached if battling parties commit themselves to an end, ideal, or a value that transcends their immediate interests. As Niebuhr observes, the "Augustinian formula for the leavening influence of a higher upon a lower loyalty or love" is a wiser and more adequate approach to changing human behavior because it appeals to love rather than law.[86] At the same time, it corrects the cynical realism of those who believe that we cannot transcend our natural selfishness. It is to be noted, once again, that the appeal to "love" is not an appeal to a temporary feeling (of pity, for instance) but to an attitude that has become a constitutive element of who we are. As Osborne puts it, love is an "attitude that changes our whole outlook and response to the object or person whom we love."[87] In a slightly different terminology, we are able to love strangers and meet their needs because we partake of a greater love that runs through the veins of a living world and that is therefore more than the sum of all individual loves.

There are two possible translations of the Augustinian insight, namely, an unprudential version and a prudential one. The leavening of loyalties to such an extent that we are capable of sacrificial self-giving is more conceivable at the interpersonal level than at the international level. But even at the collective level, the leavening power of love works through leading figures who can become exemplary figures and influence the public opinion of a nation. The articulation of higher commitments by those who influence national and international politics may effectuate a change of consciousness. This may result in justice-centered policies. In the second, prudential sense, the Augustinian formula can be understood as the extension of "self-interest" to include the interests of other parties upon which the concerned party is dependent. Policies that take the future and future generations into account result from such consideration. Another prevalent reasoning is that since we are dependent on our ecological system, its destruction will mean our destruction. We should therefore be motivated to change our consumption and production patterns, even if it means suffering some discomfort now. Such a broader and more sensible understanding of self-interest is often referred to as "self-interest rightly understood." Along this line, it can be argued that a narrow self-interest is in the long run self-defeating and is eventually detrimental to all parties concerned. Hence, a nation that is merely focused on its temporary gains estranges itself from other nations. In a global era of interdependence, such myopia boomerangs sooner or later. This means that it helps to heal the myopia of nations by demonstrating how the commitment to higher values does benefit them in the end. Of course, even such a prudential version of a leavened loyalty is not possible if the will to power is active.

NOTES

1. Strange, *Casino Capitalism*, 193.
2. Ibid, 3.
3. Schumacher, *Small is Beautiful*, 53.
4. Weil, *L'Enracinement*, 66.
5. Luc Boltanski and Eve Chiapello, *The New Spirit of Capitalism*, trans. G. Elliot (London and New York: Verso, 2007), 10.
6. Eric Schniter, Roman M. Sheremeta, and Daniel Sznycer, "Building and Rebuilding Trust with Promises and Apologies," *Journal of Economic Behavior and Organization*, 94 (2013): 242–256.
7. OECD, *Government at a Glance 2013* (Paris: OECD Publishing, 2013), https://doi.org/10.1787/gov_glance-2013-en.
8. OECD, *Government at a Glance 2019* (Paris: OECD Publishing, 2019), 13, https://doi.org/10.1787/8ccf5c38-en.
9. Ibid, 9.
10. For a definition of neoliberalism, see Bourdieu, *The Social Structures of the Economy*, 11. The criticism of neoliberalism, as conceived by most writers, is the criticism of an untamed laissez-faireism. However, a few voices have also pointed to the allegedly "older" meaning of neoliberalism, namely, a correction (and taming) of the original laissez-faire liberalism. Such history might be relevant in discussions regarding liberalism and its many variants but is quite futile when it comes to the prevailing phenomenon itself. The attempt to recall and restore "genuine" liberal and neoliberal ideologies is not very helpful since even the best versions are in need of correction.
11. Hans Jonas, *The Gnostic Religion* (Boston: Beacon Press, 1958), 323.
12. Camus, *Le mythe de Sisyphe*, 18.
13. Buber, *Between Man and Man*, 140.
14. Ibid, 132.
15. Jonas, *The Gnostic Religion*, 323.
16. Coyle, for instance, writes that "conversations with people working in the financial markets in the twelve months after Lehman Brothers 'fell over' [. . .] made it plain that Planet Banking is in a different universe to Earth [. . .] They argue that bonuses are essential to attract the best talent and stay competitive, despite the evidence that bonuses incentivized excessive risk-taking rather than productive effort." Coyle, *The Economics of Enough*, 88.

17. Casey Blake and Christopher Phelps, "History as social criticism: Conversations with Christopher Lasch," *The Journal of American History* 80, no. 4 (1994): 1132.

18. Alain Badiou and Nicolas Truong, *Éloge de l'amour* (Paris: Flammarion, 2009), 22.

19. Adler, *Understanding Human Nature*, 70.

20. Robert Skidelsky, "Afterword," in Keynes, *The General Theory of Employment, Interest, and Money*, 374.

21. Adler, *Understanding Human Nature*, 218.

22. Niebuhr, *Faith and Politics*, 18.

23. The complexity of "piety" or "pietas" is addressed in Joseph Harp Britton, *Abraham Heschel and the Phenomenon of Piety* (New York and London: Bloomsbury, 2013).

24. Cicero, *On the Republic*, 119 (Book VI, 19).

25. Ibid, 117 (Book VI, 17).

26. Ibid, 119 (Book VI, 19).

27. Cf. Jonas, *The Gnostic Religion*, 339.

28. This is what Taylor means when he says that human selves necessarily find themselves in a moral space. See, for instance, Taylor, *Sources of the Self*, 28.

29. Niebuhr, *Christianity and Power Politics*, 177–178.

30. Weil, *Attente de Dieu*, 79.

31. Simone Weil, *Cahiers II* (Paris: Plon, 1953), 239.

32. Weil, *L'Enracinement*, 61.

33. Simone Weil, *Cahiers III* (Paris: Plon, 1956), 217.

34. Niebuhr *Faith and Politics*, 69.

35. Niebuhr, *Love and Justice*, 49.

36. Buber, *A Believing Humanism*, 115.

37. Niebuhr, *Faith and Politics*, 69.

38. I argue elsewhere, in agreement with the Italian philosopher Marcello Pera, that it is possible for the nonbeliever to live out certain "religious" ideas without adhering to any institutional religion. The idea that love and justice are real, in the absolute sense of constituting reality, has been articulated by religious traditions, but it does not belong exclusively to any one of them. That idea is no longer "merely" an idea (or illusion) when it is embodied in our ordinary lives. See Roshnee Ossewaarde-Lowtoo, "A Fourth Way: Joseph Ratzinger's veluti si Deus daretur," *Gregorianum* 99, no. 1 (2018): 45–66.

39. Skidelsky and Skidelsky, *How Much is Enough?*, 218.

40. Mumford, *Technics and Civilization*, 391.

41. Cf. Arendt, *The Human Condition*, 134.

42. That said, it is significant that countless Western businesses have moved their industrial plants to the non-Western parts of the world, where these more humane conditions do not apply.

43. Cf. Polanyi, "Our Obsolete Market Mentality," 111.

44. Ibid.

45. Arendt, *The Human Condition*, 107.

46. Ibid.

47. Arendt explains: "The ideals of the homo faber, the fabricator of the world [. . .] are permanence, stability, and durability"; while "abundance [is] the ideal of the animal laborans." Ibid, 126.

48. Polanyi, "Our Obsolete Market Mentality," 115.

49. Charles Péguy, *De Jean Coste* (Paris: Gallimard, 1937), 17.

50. Polanyi, "Our Obsolete Market Mentality," 112.

51. Simone Weil, *La Pesanteur et la Grâce* (Paris: Plon, 1948), 180.

52. The use of slaves and child labor in the production of shrimps for European markets has been widely documented since 2015. See, for instance, Terre des Hommes' Child Labour Report 2015, accessed April 30, 2021, https://resourcecentre.savethechildren.net/node/13901/pdf/shrimp-study-eng-3mb.pdf.

53. Cf. Jacqueline C. Vischer, "The Effects of the Physical Environment on Job Performance: Towards a Theoretical Model of Workspace Stress," *Stress and Health* 23, no. 3. (2007): 175–184.

54. These worldwide dehumanizing practices have been documented by Human Rights Watch, among others. The reports are available at https://www.hrw.org/. See also Corey A. Ciocchetti, "The Eavesdropping Employer: A Twenty-First Century Framework for Employee Monitoring," *American Business Law Journal* 48, no. 2 (2011): 285–369; Patrick M. Sheridan "Company Limits Bathroom Breaks to 6 Minutes a Day," *CNN Business*, July 15, 2014, accessed April 30, 2021, https://money.cnn.com/2014/07/15/smallbusiness/bathroom-time-penalty/.

55. See, for instance, Jesper Starn, "A Power Plant Is Burning H&M Clothes Instead of Coal," *Bloomberg*, November 24, 2017, accessed April 30, 2021, https://www.bloomberg.com/news/articles/2017-11-24/burning-h-m-rags-is-new-black-as-swedish-plant-ditches-coal.

56. Mumford, *Technics and Civilization*, 411.

57. All technology, including digital technology and internet, has a physical (industrial) component to it even if users only get to see the virtual part of it. Primary materials are thus always involved at some point of the manufacturing line. Similarly, there is always the problem of product disposal.

58. In the case of nuclear power plants, we cannot even speak of disposal since they cannot be safely destroyed.

59. Schumacher, *Small is Beautiful*, 33.

60. Buber, *Between Man and Man*, 35.

61. OECD, *Trust and Public Policy: How Better Governance Can Help Rebuild Public Trust* (Paris: OECD Publishing, 2017), https://doi.org/10.1787/9789264268920-en; OECD, *Government at a Glance 2019.*

62. Bourdieu, *The Social Structures of the Economy*, 232.

63. Martin Buber, *Paths in Utopia*, trans. R.F.C. Hull (London: Routledge & Kegan Paul, 1949), 137.

64. Lasch, *The Revolt of the Elites*, 25–26.

65. Cicero, *On the Republic*, 47 (Book I, 39).

66. Marcus Tullius Cicero, *Laelius: On Friendship and The Dream of Scipio*, edited and translated by J.G.F. Powell (Warminster: Aris & Phillips Ltd, 1990), 41 (VIII, 26), 73 (XXVII, 100).

67. Marcus Tullius Cicero, "On the Laws," in *On the Republic and On the Laws*, trans. David Fott (Ithaca: Cornell University Press, 2014), 139 (Book I, 28).

68. Cicero, "On the Republic," 55–56 (Book I, 60).

69. Cicero, "On the Laws," 147 (Book I, 50–51).

70. Scipio discusses the three types of Republic, namely, ruled by the King, aristocrats and the people, respectively. He notes that all three "have their own separate defects. [. . .] Then they have other related, ruinous defects. In fact there is no type of republic that does not have a steep, slippery path to a neighboring bad condition." Cicero, *On the Republic*, 49 (Book I, 44). Hence, though the kingly republic, according to Scipio, "excels the others by far, [. . .] one that has been brought to a condition of equilibrium, and tempered from the three primary modes of republics, will excel the kingly one itself." Ibid, 60 (Book I, 69).

71. Cicero, *On the Republic*, 50, 52 (Book I, 45, 51–52).

72. Cicero, *On the Laws*, 193 (Book III, 32).

73. Marcus Tullius Cicero, *On Duties*, trans. Benjamin Patrick Newton (Ithaca: Cornell University Press, 2016), 57 (Book I, 85–86).

74. Cicero, *On Duties*, 99 (Book II, 33–34).

75. Buber, *Paths in Utopia*, 144.

76. Cicero, *On Duties*, 51 (Book I, 74).

77. Jean-Jacques Rousseau, "Mélanges de littérature et de morale," in *Œuvres complètes de Jean-Jacques Rousseau II*, eds. Bernard Gagnebin and Marcel Raymond (Paris: Editions Gallimard, 1964), 1273.

78. Ibid, 1277–1280.

79. Louis XIV obviously did not appreciate Fénelon's criticism of the despotism of absolute monarchs.

80. Jean Chas and Briand Pierre-César, *Nouvelle Vie De Messire François De Salignac De La Mothe Fénelon* (Paris: Chez Briand, 1788), 28–31.

81. Ibid, 33.

82. François de Salignac de La Mothe-Fénelon, *Les aventures de Télémaque, fils d'Ulysse* (Paris: Garnier-Flammarion, 1968), 478 (Book XVII). All translations are the author's.

83. Ibid, 504–505 (Book XVIII). I have translated "les peuples" as "the peoples." In the Smollett English edition, "Aimez les peuples" is translated as "love your people." It is more likely that Fénelon does mean all peoples ("nations") since he could have written "aimez votre peuple" if he meant one people. See François de Salignac de La Mothe-Fénelon, *The Adventures of Telemachus, the Son of Ulysses*, translated by Tobias Smollett and edited by Leslie A Chilton and O. M Brack (Athens, GA: University of Georgia Press, 1997), 300 (Book XXIV).

84. Mumford, *Technics and Civilization*, 85.

85. Niebuhr, *Christian Realism and Political Problems*, 110–111.

86. Ibid, 127.

87. Osborne, *Eros Unveiled*, 219.

Epilogue

The Value of Literary Utopias

The reader will probably have noticed that I have referred quite frequently to those dialogues of Plato and Cicero that could be considered as the most "utopian" because they deal with an ideal and fictive city-state that cannot, and in most cases, ought not to, be approximated in real life. The same can be said of the various well-governed nations in Fénelon's *Télémaque* and of Rousseau's ideal Republic. Why bother reading such works at all when our politico-economic problems are so much "real" and urgently require "realistic" solutions? Isn't it much more instructive to re-visit existing scholarship, evaluate them, add to them, recast them, and re-adapt them to our context? This is one way of addressing socioeconomic questions, to which I certainly have had recourse in the previous chapters. However, such an approach raises a pertinent question, namely, when do proposals count as realistic and when do they become hopelessly idealistic (in the non-philosophical sense)? Judgement is here involved. Such judgement is informed by practical experience, knowledge of human nature, and political and economic history (or more precisely, a reading of that history). Those who preach, and have recourse to, revolutions have come to the conclusion that things do not change through reasoning and persuasion. No one willingly gives up power. Coercion seems to be necessary. There is another group of people who believe that reason and compassion do not play major roles in politics and economics, and yet, they eschew revolutions. They are the "realists" who sometimes turn into cynics because they have lost hope and faith in humans. They see that revolutions do more harm than good, create new hierarchies, and merely shift power into different hands.

The faith or lack of faith in humans is not only prompted by our particular reading of history. Whether we consider radical change to be desirable, possible or not depends on our ideas and images of the human (who are we, what is proper to us humans, what are our moral possibilities and dangerous inclinations?) and of our relations to nature and the universe. Our conceptualization of the nature of moral and social changes (what are the forces of change in human life and history?) and of the causes of corruption plays a role in our considerations when we evaluate a proposal. Our judgement is also influenced by less rational considerations, of which we may not even be aware. These are both personal and cultural habits of the heart and mind. We are so used to taking certain institutions, practices, and ways of thinking and perceiving things for granted that we cannot think, feel, see, and imagine differently. We cannot imagine ourselves in a different world, different roles and leading radically different lives. Of course, the fear of the unknown, of discomfort, and of losing our social status plays a big role. But we are also, to borrow Taylor's (and Wittgenstein's) terminology, "captured by a picture."[1] This is where literary utopias come in. I believe they can set us free from our captivity by enabling us to see the picture that is captivating us. As long as we are enthralled by it, we cannot see that it is preventing us from perceiving and imagining other dimensions of reality, alternatives, and possibilities. There is no "picture" but simply our reality, which is the only reality. Literary utopias, like poetry and art, may be more powerful than arguments because they do not only appeal to our reason but instead disturb us if we are receptive to them. Literary utopias can have a similar effect on us as when we expose ourselves to a totally different civilization.

The term "utopia" appears to have been coined by Thomas More, referring to an island where the ideal commonwealth had been realized.[2] It evokes both the notions of the "perfect place" and of "no place" (*ou-topos*), the former being more recent than the latter association.[3] I am using the term "literary utopias" as opposed to more practical utopias (that include a plan of how to bring about the new world, usually through revolutions). In this sense, the dialogues of Plato and Cicero are more literary than practical even though they pertain to political philosophy. The same can be said of Rousseau since he never advocated revolutions and, in fact, did not have much hope that corrupted social conditions could be healed. The literary genre of Thomas More's *Utopia* and Fénelon's *Télémaque* is more obvious. Utopias are clearly not simply fiction. Both More's and Fénelon's novels combine fiction and epic poetry (Homer's Odyssey) with philosophy (Plato and Cicero), while implicitly alluding to their real worlds plagued by injustice and tyranny. Their commitments to certain standards of justice and their condemnation of certain conditions shine through even if we can never be completely sure whether they agree with the protagonists. Their portraits of human nature, of human passions, and of the forces that shape history – including "fate," that is, all that which escapes human control—are not inferior to treatises or empirical research. On the contrary, they surpass these in many respects because they do not suffer from the restraint of methods and the rules of logic or non-contradiction. Is the literary utopia a way of making "the truth slip more pleasantly into the mind like medicine smeared with honey?"[4] Or, is it like Paul Ricoeur says, "fancy [that] borders on madness" and hence "escapism?"[5] There are more reasons for having recourse to the utopian genre. In the case of Fénelon (and More), an open criticism of their Kings would not have had the desired results. The fictive form of *Télémaque* did not prevent Louis XIV from seeing a criticism of his rule and from punishing Fénelon. A more positive reason for the literary genre of *Télémaque* is of course its pedagogical value.

The reasons why authors have recourse to utopias are the reasons why literary utopias may be of great value to us today. So, what are their effects on us and how do (or can) they make a difference to the debates about politico-economic reforms? Their strangeness or madness can elicit two types of reaction from us. We can reject them as nonsensical. Or they can destabilize us by showing us a different way of life, even if we do not wish to embrace it. These are the reactions to alterity in general. We can choose to ignore and condemn it, or we can choose to engage with it, be it critically. Moreover, due to the strangeness of the utopia, it is not easily appropriated. In other words, while shattering our previous picture, it does not allow itself to become a new picture. What Jerry Harp says on this matter in his *Afterword* to Thomas More's *Utopia* fittingly captures what I am trying to say:

> Utopia is a nowhere that opens into new discursive spaces. Were the realm of the present and pragmatic concern to dominate entirely, we would be led into stagnation. The nowhere of Utopia—the work as well as the genre and mode of thinking—provides one way to keep consciousness on the move even though it is an impossible place (even the mathematical dimensions of the island cannot work out).[6]

Literary utopias are the manifestations of the human spirit and its idealism, without which humans would cease to be humans. What Karl Mannheim said of (practical) utopias can be applied to literary utopias: "The disappearance of utopia brings about a static state of affairs in which man himself becomes no more than a thing."[7]

In one of his lectures, Ricoeur says to be attracted precisely to what he sees as the paradox in Mannheim, namely, "that what characterizes utopia is not an inability to be actualized but a claim to shatter. The capacity of utopia to break through the thickness of reality."[8] Ricoeur is here referring to practical utopias. Literary utopias, according to him, are too much of a flight from reality. Hence, he notes that More's utopia "may provide a critical tool for undermining reality, but it is also a refuge against reality."[9] The latter claim is disputable. Instead, I think that the "unrealism" of literary utopias constitutes their very strength. By not directly attacking what we cherish, they gently remind us of the other ends of human life that we have forsaken. They mediate between realism and idealism, as it appears in the first book of *Utopia*. The dialogue between Raphael Hythloday and Thomas More illustrates the clash between "realism" and "idealism," More being the realist and Hythloday the idealist (who has lived on Utopia for a few years). Hythloday remarks that if he were to tell powerful men (such as kings) that they ought to be more concerned about the welfare of their people and not let them starve to death, no one would listen to him. More confirms this surmise of his, adding,

> And, to tell you the truth, I don't think you should obtrude such speeches or give advice which you are certain they will never accept. For how can it do any good or how can such an odd discourse influence the thinking of those whose minds are prejudiced and dead set against such notions?[10]

Truth, both men agree, will not be received by those in positions of power. In the rest of the dialogue, the clash between realism and idealism (or, more exactly, philosophy) is made painfully clear. More, the realist, notes that "if you cannot turn something to good at least make it as little bad as you can."[11]

The realist's advice to play the game and not to disrupt the whole performance pertains to the realm of action. In the realm of thought and words, more is possible. The literary utopia enables the strange truth to be told without directly upsetting the prevailing order. In this sense, it is a gentler medicine than a revolution but still a medicine. I will illustrate this argument by examining a few passages from *Utopia* and *Télémaque*, where the two major causes of injustice (private property and money) are exposed. Adoam (a Phoenician) tells Telemachus and Mentor about Baetica, the best of all well-governed commonwealths:

> All goods are held in common; the fruit of the trees and of the earth, the milk of herds and flocks, are such plentiful riches that peoples so sober and temperate do not need to divide them. Every family, being nomadic in this beautiful country, carries its tents from one place to another, after exhausting the fruits and pasturage of the spot where it had pitched its tents. Thus, having no conflicting interests that divide them, they love one another with a brotherly love that nothing can disturb.[12]

Since they do not engage in trade with other countries, they have no need of money. They give away their surpluses as gifts to other nations. Yet, there are mines of gold and silver in Baetica:

> The inhabitants, simple in their manners, and happy in their simplicity, do not reckon them as any part of their wealth; they only esteem that which truly fulfils the needs of man. [. . .] We have found gold and silver put to the same use as iron, for instance, for making ploughshares.[13]

On Utopia, too, all goods are held in common. Everyone who can work works according to his (her) own capacity and contributes to the common good, which includes a common stock of goods.

> The products of each household are taken to designated houses there and each kind of goods is separately stored in a warehouse. From them each head of household goes to get whatever he and his household need, and he takes away whatever he wants, paying no money and giving absolutely nothing in exchange for it. For why should he be denied anything, since there is plenty of everything and no one need fear that anyone would want to ask for more than he needs? For why should anyone be suspected of asking for too much if he is certain he will never lack for anything?[14]

As far as houses are concerned, they are all the same, and moreover, the inhabitants exchange houses among themselves by drawing lots every ten years.[15] Citizens to whom agricultural land is allocated—on a temporary basis—consider themselves as "tenant-farmers" instead of landlords.[16]

The Utopians export their surpluses to other nations, accepting especially iron, gold, and silver in exchange. The gold and silver are not used as money on Utopia itself since there are no monetary transactions but kept as a protection against events. The Utopians have a notable manner of "storing" these metals:

> They use gold and silver, not only in the common halls but also in private houses, to make all the chamberpots and lowliest containers. Moreover, the chains and heavy shackles used to restrain the slaves are made of the same metals. Finally, the most notorious criminals wear gold rings in their ears, gold rings on their fingers, a gold collar around their necks, and even a gold band around their heads.[17]

The Utopians are well aware of the unnatural value that is attached to gold and silver in other nations, and they thus consciously put these metals to uses that are more appropriate to their nature. "Nature," Hythloday remarks, "made the most useful elements openly available, like air, water, and earth, but she hid away what is vain and unprofitable in the most remote recesses."[18]

Our initial or instinctive reaction to the above passages might be defensive. We usually dismiss such stories as some avant la lettre "communism."

We could try to be less defensive and refrain from labelling them as communism. As soon as we give otherness a name, we reduce it to our known categories and forgo the opportunity of seeing new aspects of a boundless reality. We could also try to understand why we react so strongly to such stories. What do they confront us with? Why do we condemn them so quickly? Clearly, they undermine what we value so much, and in doing so, they clash with our self-understanding. The idea that individual efforts are not rewarded might be the hardest to accept. Why? Perhaps because work and individual achievements have become ways to earn recognition and to distinguish ourselves from others? This would mean that we fear to become anonymous, faceless, and insignificant. But isn't it deeply troubling that we only feel and experience our individuality and our "worth" through our individual productivity and individual achievements that are rewarded? Yet, neither individuality nor the diversity of humankind is denied or suppressed in these two stories. There is individual freedom, but that freedom is not the "freedom" to make profits. It is the freedom to develop ourselves, physically, intellectually, and spiritually. It is the freedom to determine our own needs but in such a way that the needs of our fellow beings are not neglected. It is the freedom to enjoy the simple pleasures of life with other fellow beings. Some Utopians may prefer to spend their free time practicing their trades, and they are free to do. Instead of getting money for those hours spent on work, they are "praised for doing so, since their labor contributes to the common good."[19]

Note that I am not defending the Utopians' and Baeticans' economic arrangements, but I am merely trying to articulate the opinions that might be impeding us from choosing the institutions that would prevent some from drowning in luxury and others from dying in destitution. If the true reason behind our dismissal of the ideals of fellowship and justice portrayed above is indeed the fear of losing our individuality, individual worth, or power, then we must urgently re-examine our self-understanding, the meaning that we attribute to work, achievements and consumption. In doing so, we will set ourselves free from enthralling pictures and pave the way for justice and civic friendship. We will also effectively address the problem of existential insecurity, which is clearly inexistent on Utopia and in Baetica. Good opinions precede good practices. Literary utopias can help us change our most tenacious opinions and habits.

NOTES

1. As Taylor points out, "We can sometimes be completely captured by a picture, not even able to imagine what an alternative would look like; or we can be

in somewhat better shape: capable of seeing that there is another way of construing things, but still having great difficulty making sense of it." Taylor, *A Secular Age*, 549.

2. The island is named after his founder Utopus. Thomas More, *Utopia*, trans. Clarence H Miller (New Haven, CT: Yale University Press, 2014), 53.

3. Cf. Jerry Harp, "Afterword," in More, *Utopia*, 146.

4. More, *Utopia*, 138.

5. Paul Ricoeur, *Lectures on Ideology and Utopia* (New York: Columbia University Press, 1986), 310.

6. Harp, "Afterword," 147.

7. Karl Mannheim, *Ideology and Utopia: An Introduction to the Sociology of Knowledge* (London: Routledge & Kegan Paul, 1954), 236.

8. Ricoeur, *Lectures on Ideology and Utopia*, 309.

9. Ibid.

10. More, *Utopia*, 43.

11. Ibid, 45.

12. Fénelon, *Les aventures de Télémaque*, 207 (Book VII).

13. Ibid, 205.

14. More, *Utopia*, 67–68.

15. Ibid, 57.

16. Ibid, 54.

17. Ibid, 76.

18. Ibid, 75.

19. Ibid, 62.

Bibliography

Adler, Alfred. "The Feeling of Inferiority and the Striving for Recognition." Translated by Walter Béran Wolfe. *Journal of the Royal Society of Medicine* 20, no. 12 (1927): 1881–1886.

———. *Understanding Human Nature*. New York: Greenberg Publisher, 1946.

Arendt, Hannah. *The Human Condition*. Chicago and London: The University of Chicago Press, 1958.

———. *Eichmann in Jerusalem: A Report on the Banality of Evil*. London: Penguin Books, 2006.

Aristotle. *Nicomachean Ethics*. Translated by H. Rackham. Cambridge, MA: Harvard University Press, 1926.

Atkins, E. Margaret, and Robert J. Dodaro, eds. *Augustine: Political Writings*. Cambridge: Cambridge University Press, 2004.

Augustine, Saint. *Commentary on the Lord's Sermon on the Mount with Seventeen Related Sermons*. Translated by Denis J. Kavanagh. Catholic University of America Press, 2001.

———. *The City of God. Books I-VII*. Translated by Demetrius B. Zema and Gerald Groveland Walsh. Washington, DC: Catholic University of America Press, 2008.

———. *The City of God. Books VIII-XVI*. Translated by Gerald G. Walsh and Grace Monahan. Washington, DC: Catholic University of America Press, 2008.

———. *The City of God. Books XVII-XXII*. Translated by Daniel J. Honan and Gerald Groveland Walsh. Washington, DC: Catholic University of America Press, 2008.

———. *Confessions*. Vol. I, Books 1–8. Translated and edited by Carolyn J.-B. Hammond. Cambridge, MA: Harvard University Press, 2014.

Badiou, Alain, and Nicolas Truong. *Éloge de l'amour*. Paris: Flammarion, 2009.

Blake, Casey, and Christopher Phelps. "History as Social Criticism: Conversations with Christopher Lasch." *The Journal of American History* 80, no. 4 (1994): 1310–1332.

Boltanski, Luc, and Eve Chiapello. *The New Spirit of Capitalism*. Translated by G. Elliot. London and New York: Verso, 2007.

Bourdieu, Pierre. *Masculine Domination*. Translated by Richard Nice. Stanford, CA: Stanford University Press, 2001.

———. *The Social Structures of the Economy*. Translated by Chris Turner. Cambridge/Malden, MA: Polity, 2008.

Boyd, Craig A., ed. *Visions of Agapé: Problems and Possibilities in Human and Divine Love*. Hampshire: Ashgate, 2008.

Britton, Joseph Harp. *Abraham Heschel and the Phenomenon of Piety*. New York and London: Bloomsbury, 2013.

Bruni, Luigino, and Anouk Grevin. *L'économie silencieuse*. Bruyères-le-Châtel: Nouvelle Cité, 2016.

Buber, Martin. *Between Man and Man*. Translated by R. G. Smith. London: Kegan Paul, 1947.

———. *Paths in Utopia*. Translated by R.F.C. Hull. London: Routledge & Kegan Paul, 1949.

———. *Pointing the Way: Collected Essays*. Translated and edited by Maurice Friedman. New York: Harper & Brothers, 1957.

———. *A Believing Humanism: My Testament 1902-1965*. Translated by Maurice Friedman. New Jersey and London: Humanities Press International, Inc., 1990.

———. *The Way of Man*. Oxford: Routledge, 1994.

———. *I and Thou*. Translated by R. G. Smith. London: Bloomsbury, 2013.

Buber, Martin, and Maurice Friedman. "Interrogation of Martin Buber." In *Philosophical Interrogations: Interrogations of Martin Buber, John Wild, Jean Wahl, Brand Blanshard, Paul Weiss, Charles Hartshorne, Paul Tillich*, edited by Sydney C. Rome and Beatrice K. Rome, 13–118. New York: Holt, Rinehart and Winston, 1964.

Burt, Donald X. *Friendship and Society: An Introduction to Augustine's Practical Philosophy*. Grand Rapids, Michigan and Cambridge, UK: William B. Eerdmans Publishing Company, 1999.

Camus, Albert. *Le mythe de Sisyphe: Essai sur l'absurde*. Paris: Gallimard, 1942.

Carden, Art, and Deirdre Nansen McCloskey. "The Bourgeois Deal: Leave Me Alone, and I'll Make You Rich." *SSRN*, March 8, 2018. http://dx.doi.org/10.2139/ssrn.3155530.

Carter, Angie, and Ahna Kruzic. "Centering the Commons, Creating Space for the Collective: Ecofeminist# NoDAPL Praxis in Iowa." *Journal of Social Justice* 7 (2017): 1–22.

Chas, Jean, and Briand Pierre-César. *Nouvelle Vie De Messire François De Salignac De La Mothe Fénelon*. Paris: Chez Briand, 1788.

Chertkovskaya, Ekaterina, Alexander Paulsson, and Stefania Barca, eds. *Towards a Political Economy of Degrowth*. London: Rowman & Littlefield International, 2019.

Cicero, Marcus Tullius. *Laelius: On Friendship and The Dream of Scipio*. Translated and edited by J.G.F. Powell. Warminster: Aris & Phillips Ltd, 1990.

———. *On the Republic and On the Laws*. Translated by David Fott. Ithaca: Cornell University Press, 2014.

———. *On Duties*. Translated by Benjamin Patrick Newton. Ithaca: Cornell University Press, 2016.

Ciocchetti, Corey A. "The Eavesdropping Employer: A Twenty-First Century Framework for Employee Monitoring." *American Business Law Journal* 48, no. 2 (2011): 285–369.

Clark, Mary T. "Augustine on Justice." *Revue d'Etudes Augustiniennes et Patristiques* 9, no. 1–2 (1963): 87–94.

Coyle, Diane. *The Economics of Enough: How to Run the Economy as if the Future Matters.* Princeton and Oxford: Princeton University Press, 2011.

Elshtain, Jean Bethke. *Democracy on Trial.* New York: BasicBooks, 1995.

England, Paula. "The Separative Self: Androcentric Bias in Neoclassical Assumptions." In *Beyond Economic Man: Feminist Theory and Economics*, edited by Marianne A. Ferber and Julie A Nelson, 37–53. Chicago: University of Chicago Press, 1993.

Entrekin, Sally, Michelle Evans-White, Brent Johnson, and Elisabeth Hagenbuch. "Rapid Expansion of Natural Gas Development Poses a Threat to Surface Waters." *Frontiers in Ecology and the Environment* 9, no. 9 (2011): 503–511.

Esteva, Gustavo, and Madhu Suri Prakash. *Grassroots Postmodernism: Remaking the Soil of Cultures.* London: Zed Books, 2014.

Fénelon, François de Salignac de La Mothe. *Les aventures de Télémaque, fils d'Ulysse.* Paris: Garnier-Flammarion, 1968.

———. *The Adventures of Telemachus, the Son of Ulysses.* Translated by Tobias Smollett and edited by Leslie A. Chilton and O. M. Brack. Athens, GA: University of Georgia Press, 1997.

Friedman, Maurice. *My Friendship with Martin Buber.* New York: Syracuse University Press, 2013.

Gagnebin, Bernard, and Marcel Raymond, eds. *Œuvres complètes de Jean-Jacques Rousseau I.* Paris: Editions Gallimard, 1959.

———, eds. *Œuvres complètes de Jean-Jacques Rousseau II.* Paris: Editions Gallimard, 1964.

———, eds. *Œuvres complètes de Jean-Jacques Rousseau III.* Paris: Editions Gallimard, 1964.

———, eds. *Œuvres complètes de Jean-Jacques Rousseau IV.* Paris: Editions Gallimard, 1969.

Giljum, Stefan, Friedrich Hinterberger, Martin Bruckner, Eva Burger, Johannes Frühmann, Stephan Lutter, Elke Pirgmaier, Christine Polzin, Hannes Waxwender, Lisa Kernegger, and Michael Warhurst. "Overconsumption: Our Use of the World's Natural Resources." Friends of the Earth International, September 3, 2009. Accessed April 30, 2021. https://www.foei.org/resources/publications/publications-by-subject/economic-justice-resisting-neoliberalism-publications/overconsumption-our-use-of-the-worlds-natural-resources.

Gray, John. *Straw Dogs: Thoughts on Humans and Other Animals.* London: Granta Books, 2002.

Grotius, Hugo. *Commentary on the Law of Prize and Booty*, edited by Martine Julia van Ittersum. Indianapolis: Liberty Fund, 2006.

Hallam, Kate. "Environmental Defenders: Murdered, Missing and At Risk." *Socialist Lawyer* 75 (2017): 40–43. https://doi.org/10.13169/socialistlawyer.75.0040.

Hamilton, Clive. *Defiant Earth: The Fate of Humans in the Anthropocene*. Cambridge: Polity Press, 2017.

Harp, Jerry. "Afterword." In Thomas More. *Utopia*. Translated by Clarence H. Miller, 172–191. New Haven, CT: Yale University Press, 2014.

Hengstmengel, Joost. *Divine Providence in Early Modern Economic Thought*. London and New York: Routledge, 2019.

Heschel, Abraham J. *Man is Not Alone: A Philosophy of Religion*. New York: Farrar, Strauss & Giroux, 1951.

———. *Who is Man?* Stanford, CA: Stanford University Press, 1965.

Hirschfeld, Mary L. *Aquinas and the Market: Toward a Humane Economy*. Cambridge, MA and London: Harvard University Press, 2018.

Hodgson, Louise. *Res Publica and the Roman Republic: "Without Body or Form"*. Oxford: Oxford University Press, 2016.

Holsclaw, Geoffrey. *Society and Freedom, in Transcending Subjects: Augustine, Hegel, and Theology*. Chichester: John Wiley & Sons Ltd, 2016.

Horkheimer, Max, and Theodor Adorno. *Dialectic of Enlightenment: Philosophical Fragments*. Translated by Edmund Jephcott and edited by Gunzelin Schmid Noerr. Stanford, CA: Stanford University Press, 2002.

Illich, Ivan. *In the Mirror of the Past: Lectures and Addresses 1978-1990*. New York and London: Marion Boyars, 1992.

Ittersum, Martine Julia van. "Hugo Grotius in Context: Van Heemskerck's Capture of the Santa Catarina and its Justification in De Jure Praedae (1604-1606)." *Asian Journal of Social Science* 31, no. 3 (2003): 511–548.

Johnson, Simon. "The Quiet Coup." *The Atlantic* 1, May 2009. Accessed April 30, 2021. https://www.theatlantic.com/magazine/archive/2009/05/the-quiet-coup/307364/.

Jonas, Hans. *The Gnostic Religion*. Boston: Beacon Press, 1958.

Kaufmann, Jean-Claude. *The Curious History of Love*. Translated by David Macey. Cambridge: Polity Press, 2011.

Keynes, John Maynard. "Economic Possibilities for Our Grandchildren (1930)." In *The Collected Writings of John Maynard Keynes*, edited by Elizabeth Johnson and Donald Moggridge, 321–332. London: Royal Economic Society, 1978.

———. *The General Theory of Employment, Interest, and Money*. Cham: Palgrave Macmillan, 2018.

Krugman, Paul. "Introduction." In John Maynard Keynes. *The General Theory of Employment, Interest, and Money*, xxv–xliii. Cham: Palgrave Macmillan, 2018.

Lasch, Christopher. *The Culture of Narcissism: American Life in an Age of Diminishing Expectations*. New York: W.W. Norton, 1978.

———. *The Minimal Self: Psychic Survival in Troubled Times*. London: Pan Books, 1984.

———. *The Revolt of the Elites and the Betrayal of Democracy*. New York and London: W.W. Norton & Company, 1995.

Liegey, Vincent, and Anitra Nelson. *Exploring Degrowth: A Critical Guide*. London: Pluto Press, 2020.

Lipovetsky, Gilles. *L'ère du vide: essais sur l'individualisme contemporain*. Paris: Gallimard, 1983.

Lipovetsky, Gilles, and Bertrand Richard. *La société de deception*. Paris: Textuel, 2006.

Long, Heather. "Bernie Sanders Asks If Wall Street is Necessary." *CNN Business*, April 18, 2016. Accessed April 30, 2021. https://money.cnn.com/2016/04/18/investing/bernie-sanders-new-york-wall-street/index.html.

Lyotard, Jean-François, *Moralités Postmodernes*. Paris: Galilée, 1993.

Maclure, Jocelyn, and Charles Taylor. *Secularism and Freedom of Conscience*. Cambridge, MA: Harvard University Press, 2011.

Manne, Anne. *The Life of I: The New Culture of Narcissism*. Melbourne University Press, 2014.

Mannheim, Karl. *Ideology and Utopia: An Introduction to the Sociology of Knowledge*. London: Routledge & Kegan Paul, 1954.

Marcel, Gabriel. *The Decline of Wisdom*. New York: Philosophical Library, 1955.

Marcuse, Herbert. *One-Dimensional Man: Studies in the Ideology of Advanced Industrial Society*. London and New York: Routledge, 1964.

———. *Eros and Civilization: A Philosophical Inquiry into Freud*. Boston: Beacon Press, 1966.

Maritain, Jacques. *Christianity and Democracy and the Rights of Man and Natural Law*. Translated by Doris C. Anson. San Francisco: Ignatius Press, 1986.

Maslow, Abraham H. "A Theory of Human Motivation." *Psychological Review* 50, no. 4 (1943): 370–396.

McCloskey, Deirdre. "Bourgeois Towns: How Capitalism Became Virtuous, 1600-1776," December 19, 2007. Accessed January 15, 2020. https://cadmus.eui.eu/.

McCloskey, Deirdre N. *The Bourgeois Virtues: Ethics for an Age of Commerce*. University of Chicago Press, 2006.

McGrath, Sean J. *Thinking Nature: An Essay in Negative Ecology*. Edinburgh: Edinburgh University Press, 2019.

More, Thomas. *Utopia*. Translated by Clarence H. Miller. New Haven, CT: Yale University Press, 2014.

Mumford, Lewis. *Technics and Civilization*. New York and Burlingame: Harcourt, Brace & World, Inc., 1963.

Murdoch, Iris. *The Sovereignty of Good*. New York: Schocken Books, 1971.

Murphy, Sophia, David Burch, and Jennifer Clapp. "Cereal Secrets: The World's Largest Grain Traders and Global Agriculture." *Oxfam Research Reports*, August 3, 2012. Accessed April 30, 2021. https://www.oxfam.org/en/research/cereal-secrets-worlds-largest-grain-traders-and-global-agriculture.

Niebuhr, Reinhold. *Christian Realism and Political Problems*. London: Faber and Faber, 1954.

———. *An Interpretation of Christian Ethics*. New York: Meridian Books, 1956.

———. *Love and Justice: Selections from the Shorter Writings of Reinhold Niebuhr*, edited by D. B. Robertson. Louisville, KY: Westminster/John Knox Press, 1957.

———. *Moral Man and Immoral Society: A Study in Ethics and Politics*. London: SCM Press Ltd, 1963.

———. *Faith and Politics: A Commentary on Religious, Social and Political Thought in a Technological Age*, edited by Ronald H. Stone. New York: George Braziller, 1968.

———. *Christianity and Power Politics*. Hamden, CT: Archon Books, 1969.

Nussbaum, Martha C., *Love's Knowledge: Essays on Philosophy and Literature*. Oxford: Oxford University Press, 1990.

———. *Political Emotions: Why Love Matters for Justice*. Cambridge, MA and London: The Belknap Press of Harvard University Press, 2013.

OECD. *Government at a Glance 2013*. Paris: OECD Publishing, 2013. https://doi.org/10.1787/gov_glance-2013-en.

———. *Government at a Glance 2019*. Paris: OECD Publishing, 2019. https://doi.org/10.1787/8ccf5c38-en.

———. *Trust and Public Policy: How Better Governance Can Help Rebuild Public Trust*. ParisOECD Publishing, 2017. https://doi.org/10.1787/9789264268920-en.

Opdebeeck, Hendrik. *The Economy and Meaningfulness: A Utopia?* Brussels: Peter Lang, 2019.

Osborne, Catherine. *Eros Unveiled: Plato and the God of Love*. Oxford: Clarendon Press, 2002.

Ossewaarde-Lowtoo, Roshnee. "A Fourth Way: Joseph Ratzinger's veluti si Deus daretur." *Gregorianum* 99, no. 1 (2018): 45–66.

———. "Conquering Megalomania and Despair: A Niebuhrian Response to the Politico-Economic Impasse." *International Journal of Public Theology* 13, no. 3 (2019): 339–359.

Péguy, Charles. *De Jean Coste*. Paris: Gallimard, 1937.

Plato. "Gorgias." In Plato. *Lysis-Symposium-Gorgias*. Translated by W. R. M. Lamb. Cambridge, MA: Harvard University Press, 1925.

———. "Euthyphro." In Plato. *The Trial and Death of Socrates: Four Dialogues*. Translated by Benjamin Jowett. New York: Dover Publications, 1992.

———. *Republic, Volume I: Books 1-5*, edited and translated by Christopher Emlyn-Jones and William Preddy. Cambridge, MA: Harvard University Press, 2013.

———. *Republic, Volume II: Books 6-10*, edited and translated by Christopher Emlyn-Jones and William Preddy. Cambridge, MA: Harvard University Press, 2013.

Polanyi, Karl. "Our Obsolete Market Mentality: Civilization Must Find a New Thought Pattern." *Commentary* 4 (1947): 109–117.

———. *The Great Transformation: The Political and Economic Origins of Our Time*. Boston: Beacon Press, 2001.

Ricoeur, Paul. *Lectures on Ideology and Utopia*. New York: Columbia University Press, 1986.

———. *Amour et Justice*. Paris: Éditions Points, 2008.

Riley, Patrick. *Leibniz' Universal Jurisprudence: Justice as the Charity of the Wise*. Cambridge, MA: Harvard University Press, 1996.

Scheler, Max. *On Feeling, Knowing, and Valuing: Selected Writings,* edited by Harold J. Bershady. Chicago and London: The University of Chicago Press, 1992.

Sandel, Michael J. *The Tyranny of Merit: What's Become of the Common Good?* New York: Farrar, Straus and Giroux, 2020.

Schniter, Eric, Roman M. Sheremeta, and Daniel Sznycer. "Building and Rebuilding Trust with Promises and Apologies." *Journal of Economic Behavior and Organization* 94 (2013): 242–256.

Schumacher, Ernst Friedrich. *Small is Beautiful: A Study of Economics as if People Mattered.* London: Blond & Briggs, 1976.

Schutter, Olivier De. "Addressing Concentration in Food Supply Chains. The Role of Competition Law in Tackling the Abuse of Buyer Power," December 6, 2010. Accessed April 30, 2021. https://www.ohchr.org/Documents/Issues/Food/BN3_SRRTF_Competition_ENGLISH.pdf.

Sheridan, Patrick M. "*Company limits bathroom breaks to 6 minutes a day.*" *CNN Business*, July 15, 2014. Accessed April 30, 2021. https://money.cnn.com/2014/07/15/smallbusiness/bathroom-time-penalty/.

Skidelsky, Robert, and Edward Skidelsky. *How Much is Enough?: Money and the Good Life*. New York: Other Press, 2012.

Skidelsky, Robert. "Afterword." In John Maynard Keynes. *The General Theory of Employment, Interest, and Money*, 373–376. Cham: Palgrave Macmillan, 2018.

Smith, Adam. *An Inquiry into the Nature and Causes of the Wealth of Nations*, Vol. 1. Oxford: Clarendon Press, 1979.

———. *The Theory of Moral Sentiments*. Indianapolis: Liberty Fund, 1984.

South, Nigel, and Avi Brisman. "Critical Green Criminology, Environmental Rights and Crimes of Exploitation." *New Directions in Crime and Deviancy* (2013): 99–110.

Starn, Jesper. "A Power Plant Is Burning H&M Clothes Instead of Coal." *Bloomberg*, November 24, 2017. Accessed April 30, 2021. https://www.bloomberg.com/news/articles/2017-11-24/burning-h-m-rags-is-new-black-as-swedish-plant-ditches-coal.

Stern, Nicholas. *The Economics of Climate Change: The Stern Review*. Cambridge: Cambridge University Press, 2007.

Stout, Margaret. "Back to the Future: Toward a Political Economy of Love and Abundance." *Administration and Society* 42, no. 1 (2010): 3–37.

Strange, Susan. *Casino Capitalism*. Oxford: Basil Blackwell, 1986.

Taylor, Charles. *Sources of the Self: The Making of the Modern Identity*. Cambridge: Cambridge University Press, 1989.

———. "Modernity and the Rise of the Public Sphere." *The Tanner Lectures on Human Values,* edited by Grethe B. Peterson, 203–206. Salt Lake City: University of Utah Press, 1993.

———. *A Secular Age*. Cambridge MA: The Belknap Press of Harvard University Press, 2007.

Terre des Hommes. *Child Labour Report 2015*. Accessed April 30, 2021. https://resourcecentre.savethechildren.net/node/13901/pdf/shrimp-study-eng-3mb.pdf.

Tillich, Paul. *Love, Power and Justice*. Oxford: Oxford University Press, 1977.

Vazquez-Brust, Diego, Alastair M. Smith, and Joseph Sarkis. "Managing the Transition to Critical Green Growth: The 'Green Growth State'." *Futures* 64 (2014): 38–50.

Vischer, Jacqueline C. "The Effects of the Physical Environment on Job Performance: Towards a Theoretical Model of Workspace Stress." *Stress and Health* 23, no. 3 (2007): 175–184.

Vlek, Charles. "Induced Earthquakes from Long-Term Gas Extraction in Groningen, the Netherlands: Statistical Analysis and Prognosis for Acceptable-Risk Regulation." *Risk Analysis* (2018): 1455–1473.

Voltaire. *Lettres Philosophiques,* edited by Olivier Ferret and Antony McKenna. Paris: Classiques Garnier, 2010.

Watts, Jonathan, and John Vidal. "Environmental Defenders Being Killed in Record Numbers Globally, New Research Reveals." *Chain Reaction* 130, September 2017.

Weil, Simone. *La Pesanteur et la Grâce*. Paris: Plon, 1948.

———. *L'Enracinement*. Paris: Gallimard, 1949.

———. *Attente de Dieu*. Paris: La Colombe, 1950.

———. *Cahiers II*. Paris: Plon, 1953.

———. *Cahiers III*. Paris: Plon, 1956.

Wilson, Aaron Bruce. *Peirce's Empiricism: Its Roots and Its Originality*. Lanham, MD: Lexington Books, 2016.

Yohannan, Alina. "The Standing Rock Sioux Indians: An Inconvenience for the Black Gold." *Journal of Land and Development* 6 (2016): 19–31.

Index

About the Author

Roshnee Ossewaarde-Lowtoo received her doctorate in 2015 from Tilburg University, the Netherlands. She holds a bachelor's degree in economics (London School of Economics and Political Science), a master's degree in philosophy (Erasmus University of Rotterdam, the Netherlands), and a master's degree in theology (Tilburg University). The main aim of her doctoral dissertation was the articulation of a philosophical anthropology that is comprehensive enough to match and support the modern aspiration to universal justice and benevolence. To this end she studied the works of Charles Taylor, Paul Valadier, and Joseph Ratzinger. A similar exploration of the highest conceivable human goals and of the limits proper to human life characterizes her postdoctoral research on the humanization of economic realities.

www.ingramcontent.com/pod-product-compliance
Ingram Content Group UK Ltd.
Pitfield, Milton Keynes, MK11 3LW, UK
UKHW041843031026
15587UKWH00002B/982

9 781793 642103